HOCKEY'S ODYSSEY!
FROM DHYAN CHAND TO CHARLESWORTH

Trevor Vanderputt

ATHENA PRESS
LONDON

HOCKEY'S ODYSSEY!
Copyright © T Vanderputt 2003

All Rights Reserved

No part of this book may be reproduced in any form
by photocopying or by any electronic or mechanical means,
including information storage or retrieval systems,
without permission in writing from both the copyright
owner and the publisher of this book.

ISBN 1 84401 074 0

First Published 2003 by
ATHENA PRESS
Queen's House, 2 Holly Road
Twickenham TW1 4EG

Printed for Athena Press

HOCKEY'S ODYSSEY!
FROM DHYAN CHAND TO CHARLESWORTH

Dedicated to my wife Jean

Acknowledgements

The author wishes to thank all the people who contributed to this book, especially the following:

Syd Johnson, Stan Salazar, Dick Aggiss, Sid Waller, Jack Purcell, Gian Singh, Jenelle Stone, John Fonseca, Basil Sellers, Keith Matthews and the management and staff of Hockey Australia, especially Linden Adamson, the current Chief Executive Officer.

All illustrations in this book remain the property of their respective owners. The author gratefully acknowledges the cooperation of the following people and organizations in reproducing these images: *Hockey Australia*, *Thundersticks*; Pat Jansen; Richard Aggiss; Syd Johnson; Steve Purcell, Trevor Vanderputt and family.

Foreword

This book is the outcome of a lifetime of dedication to the sport of hockey.

It is one Anglo-Indian's perception of the glory days of hockey in India from the thirties to the mid-sixties.

It is a view of Australian hockey from 1964 to 1987 seen through the eyes of one who has been a Director of Coaching for the ACT Hockey Association, a member of the Glebe Hockey Club of Sydney, a coach of the Camberwell Hockey Club in Melbourne and a coach and player for the Cricketers' Hockey Club of Western Australia.

Hockey's Odyssey is my tribute to my mother country, India, once indomitable in world hockey. It is my tribute to my adoptive land, Australia, its present and future paved with hockey gold.

It is my tribute to my community, the Anglo-Indians, who brought the spirit of undefeated champions from the sub-continent to the southern hemisphere. This is their odyssey, an odyssey that continues through into the future with the girls and boys of Australia.

This is my tribute to you who trusted me to coach you to maturity over many years in the past. Your talent and courage is where true gold is to be found.

Finally, this book is a thanksgiving for a lifetime of satisfaction, a life well spent in a worthy sport, and the family and friends who made it possible. In that sense, too, this book is the chronicle of an odyssey, an intensely personal one.

Contents

Chapter One: Background and Early Days	9
Chapter Two: Overview–Dhyan Chand to Charlesworth	22
Chapter Three: Indian Hockey	49
Chapter Four: Sydney, Australia 1964	68
Chapter Five: Western Australia 1969	83
Chapter Six: Melbourne Memories 1980	128
Chapter Seven: ACT Hockey Association 1981–84	136
Australian Players 1922-1985	142

CHAPTER ONE: BACKGROUND AND EARLY DAYS

My great-grandfather was a seafarer in the Dutch East India Company. The sailing ships of those days came around the Cape of Good Hope, up into the Indian Ocean and through the Bay of Bengal on their way to the Dutch East Indies, now called Indonesia. Sometimes they would call in at a port on the East coast of India called Vizagapatnam, to refit and take on fresh food and water. On one of these trips the early Vanderputt decided to jump ship and settle in this vast new sub-continent (new to Europeans, that is!) He spent most of his early years in South India, married and had a son called Alec, who in turn married an India-born Englishwoman named Marie Milner.

In this way my Dutch ancestor joined a community often referred to as Domiciled Europeans and later as Anglo-Indians. These were people born in India of European descent, in the male line. During the earliest days of the East India Company they were mainly the offspring of unions between British soldiers and local women, and consequently they were often cruelly referred to as 'half-castes'. This was a curious term to emerge from a nation which was, itself, an indeterminate mixture of races, including Italian, Scandinavian, Spanish, Indo-European and Phoenician.

There is a point to this explanation of my genetic pool in a book about hockey. These so-called 'half-castes', the Anglo-Indians, offspring of both East and West, were, in the next two hundred and fifty years, to provide yeoman service in establishing a nation-building network of railways, telegraphs, customs, police, academic institutions, hospitals, and most importantly, armies, during the early days of the British and French rule. When there was no one left to conquer, as it is often said, the prowess of the British Empire began to be shown on the playing fields of Eton – and the hockey fields of India, by Anglo-Indians.

The girl that Vanderputt the Dutchman married was the grandchild of Colonel Henry Haversham, of Mount Godwin Austen fame. Mont[*] Everest is the highest mountain in the world, as everybody knows. The second highest is K2, as it is now known. Then it was named after Godwin Austen, the family name of Haversham, who had surveyed the K2 region for the Office of the Surveyor General of India.

Haversham was as romantic as his mountain. He married a Kashmiri woman from a wealthy family and had a daughter from the union. They named the girl Marie. When the mother died Haversham was just about to leave for Victorian England. He left his infant daughter with an English family living in India called the Milners, never failing to provide her with generous financial support from England. Marie grew up and married one of the Milner boys and a daughter was born of this marriage. They named her Marie, after her mother Marie Haversham. She married the Dutchman Vanderputt's son Alec and had three girls and one son – Edward John, my father.

Anglo-Indians were now marrying fellow Anglo-Indians and a distinct community was being formed. It became the backbone of the East India Company and later, after the Indian Mutiny of 1857, became indispensable to the British Administration that took over the ruling of India. Because

---

[*] '*Mont* Everest' is the name used by the Surveyor-General of India

of the harsh environment –heat, monsoons, flies, wild animals, snakes and warring tribes – English-born employees were scarce and got ill frequently.

Remember this was the time that railway, postal and telegraph systems were being established throughout the sub-continent. The tough jobs fell to the 'country-born', as they were known – men and women who were English in loyalty, language and culture, but who were hardy as the 'natives', knew their tongues and could get on with them. The plum jobs were reserved for the relatives of the British ruling classes. Many of them were educated in English public schools and received specialist training in Hailybury in England, an establishment set up especially for the development of the future officer cadre in the Imperial Civil Service (ICS) to serve all over the Empire.

If my great-grandparents' union smacked of all the romance of India, my parents' union was just as romantic, but rather more turbulent. My mother, Diana Rodda, was a beautiful, raven-haired, stunningly talented ballroom dancer. She was also of the Jewish faith. Her grandfather had fled persecution in the Middle East and had taken refuge in a very tolerant Hindu India at the turn of the twentieth century. A middle-class merchant, he was welcomed in Calcutta.

The tight-knit Calcutta Jewish community were shocked and outraged when one of their young women fell in love with a Christian. She was ostracized from her family and the rest of her community for breaking tradition. However, she discovered her new-found freedom from the orthodox religion she had grown up with very much to her liking, and it fitted in perfectly with her chosen career.

The rapidly emerging modern middle class in Calcutta had created a great need for schools in the 'social graces', especially the need to learn how to dance and join in the social life of the ballroom generation. My mother set up the first Diana Rodda School of Ballroom Dancing in our Park Circus house in Theatre Road. She was an instant success! With her talent as a fine ballroom dancer she was able to earn enough money to support her two little sons and a man who was in and out of permanent work. It was, of course, the start of the Great Depression.

I was born in 1931 and my brother two years later in 1933. Growing up in the middle-class suburb of Park Circus, we played hockey in the street, flew kites or roller-skated with our mates. Although we had been baptised as Catholics there was no Catholic church in Park Circus in those early days of the thirties, and we had to catch the tram to St. Teresa's church in Entally for Sunday Mass.

School was next on the agenda of life. In Calcutta, the Anglicans ran three schools, St. James, St Thomas' Boys in Free School Street and a kindergarten and school for girls at Kidderpore, a suburb in the south of Calcutta. My brother went to the Kidderpore kindergarten and I went to Free School Street. We were both free boarders as these schools were set up for the express purpose of catering to kids of families who could not afford to pay school fees due to the growing unemployment factor. The school Chaplain was a Reverend Brian. He later became Bishop of Calcutta and Bengal.

The school holidays were memorable because I spent them in 'Green Ridges', my Aunt Marie's home in Darjeeling, the wonderful hill station in the Himalayas with stunning views of the snows and the mighty Kenchinjunga. Playing in the snow, pony riding, skating, going to the Chowrasta (Main Road) to listen to the Military band on Sundays, were all magical to a nine year old!

The so-called 'Toy Train' went from the end of the main line in the plains at Siligoorie to Darjeeling via Kurseong. The view from the window was a wonderful panorama. After all this splendour I dreaded returning to

Calcutta to live with my mother and father.

My father was constantly battling to get money out of my Mum to gamble either at the races or at cards, or to spend on liquor. The brand of beer he drank was a Japanese brew called Sakura beer.

Well, my mother tolerated this rotten life for years with a man who almost never worked but continually sponged off her. She finally vowed to leave him and did so the minute he got a job. She packed up and left for New Delhi, taking my brother and myself to a new life in a new city. She set up the Diana Rodda School of Ballroom Dancing in New Delhi, and enrolled us in a paid school, St Michael's in Patna.

After two years in Kurjee (St Michael's) we were transferred to St Edwards Milsington in Simla which was more upmarket than Kurjee and closer to New Delhi, our permanent new home.

SIMLA

This beautiful hill station in the Himalayas rises about 7000 feet above sea-level. It was used by the British Government as their summer capital during the hot steamy weather in New Delhi to give their staff respite for a few months every year.

The two main schools for boys were Bishop Cotton High School, which was Anglican, and St Edwards High School, run by the Irish Christian Brothers, which was Roman Catholic. Bishop Cotton had about 250 boarders but Milsington (St Eds) had only about a hundred boarders.

Early memories of this school have always brought me a great deal of joy. The school term went from early March till the first week of December. While some felt that parents who 'locked away' their children for nine months in the year lacked love or interest in them, most of the boys really had a wonderful life experience. We learned, apart from our book studies, the art of looking after ourselves. The discipline of these boarding schools was directly responsible for the success in later life of the majority of graduates leaving these schools.

I remember the night 'raids' on the fruit orchards. The apples and other fruit were of the highest quality and being picked right off the trees were always the freshest fruit I have ever eaten then or since.

In my fourth year in St Ed's, when I was in my pre-Senior Cambridge class, I was given the honour of being appointed a prefect and House Captain. House players in the various sports teams and the younger kids looked up to prefects and gave them a degree of respect that few people ever enjoy anywhere! One's self-esteem reached an all-time high when one dealt successfully with challenging situations, whether it was bullying or loss of form on the sports field. It was a privilege to assist other kids with their problems.

In 1947, the year of Indian Independence, our hockey and football (soccer) first elevens were pretty strong. I remember well that we beat our traditional and much larger rivals, Bishop Cotton, for the first time ever in soccer that year. We were so carried away that our Principal organized a friendly inter-school match with the exclusive Military school reserved for the kids of British soldiers serving in India, a school called Lawrence Memorial (Sanawar). This was located in a hill station called Kasauli, which was halfway between Simla and Kalka at the foot of the plains. They were mainly 16 and 17-year-olds, too big and strong for us. They thrashed us and brought us down to earth!

My next memory of Simla is not pleasant. It was when the ferocious killings began in the aftermath of the Partition of British India into two new entities, India and Pakistan. Muslims in newly-formed Pakistan were attacking and killing Hindus and Sikhs on their side of the new border, which cut the rich province of Punjab into two, and Hindus and Sikhs in India were retaliating with equal ferocity and horror on Muslims trying to flee to Pakistan. The first Muslim coolie killed in Simla lost his life just outside our school gate. Fear and anxious days followed, as no one was really sure that this senseless killing would stop with the killing of Muslims only. What about other non-Hindus? Our worries were unfounded and we were grateful to be left alone.

For the following three-and-a-half months all coolies in Simla were either too scared to come out of hiding or had left for the safety of Pakistan, because they were all Muslims. The members of my school class, not having to face a formal exam at the end of the year, were used by the school to man a hand-pulled cart (like a large trailer with four wheels) to haul the daily stores for the entire school from the local bazaar on the Cart Road below the town proper, a distance of some four miles.

NAINI TAL 1948 TO LONDON 1949

The Irish Christian Brothers decided not to reopen the boarding side of St. Edwards in 1948 because of the Partition riots and the state of affairs on both sides of the new India-Pakistan border. My mother then enrolled my brother and myself into St Joseph's College in Naini Tal, a hill station in the province of the Uttar Pradesh. This was one of the more exclusive and expensive private schools in India, with only about two hundred boarders. The neighbouring Anglican Sherwood College had only about eighty boarders and very few non-British students. St Joseph's was also known as 'Sem', having been used as a Catholic seminary in the late eighteen hundreds. Three generations of the Ranas of Nepal, the ruling family, had come to 'Sem' to get their English education.

My class master was an Irishman affectionately known to

the boys as Fuzzy. His real name was Brother S. Murphy. He was particularly kind to me and my brother as he knew we were from a broken home, brought up by our mother with no father figure. For forty years after I left the College we kept in touch.

When I visited India from Australia in 1987, I returned to my Alma Mater and we were genuinely pleased to see each other again. By this time he was in his late eighties but still going strong. Sadly he died just a year later in his beloved Ireland, having suffered a stroke in India. A great man, a wonderful teacher! Among his numerous students many went on to be high officials in the Government of free India and in the Catholic Church. One was K.C. Pant (Home Minister Govind Balla Pant's son), who later became Defence Minister of India, and there are two Bishops of the Catholic Church in India and one Archbishop who proudly claim to be the ex-students of Brother S. Murphy, our beloved Fuzzy.

Well, I passed my Senior Cambridge Exam in 1948, but with insufficient grades to carry on with higher studies. I persuaded my mother to let me go to England where most of my classmates had gone. She agreed, as the future of members of our community was not considered to be bright in the new India.

In March 1949 as a seventeen-year old I sailed on the S.S. Asturia, a P&O liner that was now back on the India/UK run, having been refitted during the War to act as a troop ship. For this reason it offered cheaper fares, ideal for people trying to get to England in the aftermath of Indian Independence.

We stopped briefly at Aden, went through the Red Sea and the Suez Canal, and docked at last at the port of Southampton on the south coast of England. British Immigration wasn't terribly strict [people were not too fussed with a ship arriving after hours] in those days, and I ventured ashore at about ten thirty that evening with not one person to stop me.

My first impression was how clean everything was: no garbage in the streets, no urine smells. If this was what England was like I was really going to like the place! Next day I caught a train to Waterloo station in London where a good friend of my father's from Calcutta, Basil Anthony, met me and took me back to his home in West Ealing. While crossing the river Thames in the cab 'Uncle' Basil pointed out how narrow the river was compared to our rivers in India. Compared to the Ganges and the Brahmaputra the Thames was a mere canal!

A son of Uncle Basil's worked for the travel agents Thomas Cook and Sons in their London Head Office in Green Park, Berkeley Square, two Underground stations from Piccadilly Circus. He had organized a job interview for me and I was lucky enough to get the job – my first job ever! I was now a Junior Clerk in the Holiday Tours Department, on the princely sum of *two pounds ten shillings a week*, the junior wage, as I was under eighteen. A few months later, on my eighteenth birthday, I got a raise to *four pounds ten shillings a week*.

I loved my job and my work mates. I spent my spare time watching the Queens Park Rangers football team at the Shepherd's Bush ground until I was talked into switching my allegiance to the First Division Chelsea Football Club. Stamford Bridge ground was then my home ground. I was persuaded to go with my workmates to the Ice Hockey. They were Harrangay Racers fans and I was soon given a beanie and a scarf so I could sit with them at the games. Great entertainment these Canadian Pros provided. Well, nearly all of them were Canadian.

Jazz was my other hobby. I loved it and was a regular at the Club Eleven in Soho where they had Ronnie Scott, Johnny Dankworth, Hank Shaw and a lot of musos who were into the new music called Be-Bop. On a Monday night I went to the Palais de Dance hall in Hammersmith for the one-night stands of all the Big Bands, including Vic Lewis, Ted Heath and Tito Burns. Such wonderful memories!

In spite of having such a great time, as a young eighteen-year-old I yearned for sunny India and my family. The cold and the wet had got to me. I returned to India in early December, steaming out of Tilbury on the S.S. Stratheden, arriving in Bombay and on to New Delhi in time for Christmas 1949, much to the delight of my mother.

NEW DELHI

In January 1950 I started looking for a job in New Delhi. I was 18 years old and had only eight months' work experience with travel agents Thomas Cook in London as a junior clerk. For nearly three months I applied to all and sundry for employment. Seeking solace at the New Delhi Club one evening I was approached by a gentleman who introduced himself as Bert Cleminson, the father of a St Joseph's schoolmate of mine who had been about five classes junior to me. My young friend had told his father that I had recently returned from England and was looking for a job. Bert offered me employment which was the start of a forty-year working life, on and off, with Gestetner Ltd.

I started work on April 1st as a mechanic, learning all about duplicating machines. Luckily I had brought my BSA pushbike back from the UK with me. I was given an allowance for using it to call on customers wanting free mechanical service on their equipment.

Riding around a blazing hot Delhi in the months of May and June on a pushbike was enough to make anyone want to pack in the job, but I was convinced I had a future with this company, and stuck to my task. Then came the rains. On some occasions I was soaked to the skin while on my bike travelling to Delhi University and other far-flung Delhi suburbs of the early fifties. My employers were evidently pleased with my work and attitude. I was selected to go to the Head Office in Calcutta for training on the latest new model of duplicating machine due to be released.

In Calcutta I was trained by an Anglo-Indian called Len Taylor, who later went to England for the firm and loyally worked many years there. Come the 1st of January 1951, I was promoted to the newly-created position of 'Sales and Service Rep'. Three weeks in the month I worked in a country area in western Uttar Pradesh and one week in the month I worked in the Old Delhi area of the city.

I was so keen on my hockey and soccer that I always carried my hockey stick and boots with me whenever I was on tour so I could have some practice after the close of work for the day. Most of the time in these U.P. towns I'd travel by cycle rickshaw and stop the rickshaw wallah as soon as I saw some players either playing a practice match or just training and ask if I could join in! It never failed to get me a game.

The small Railway towns in my territory always had a Railway Institute where staff of the railways and other Anglo-Indians living in the town congregated for their entertainment or just for a social drink. The Indians referred to these Institutes as 'Natch-Ghurr' or dancing house as they're always remembered for holding dances for the Sahibs. On reaching a station or town with a decent Institute I'd put my bags in the hands of the Station Rest Room bearer and jump into a rickshaw and simply say *'Natch Ghurr Chaloe.'* Translated, it means, 'Take me to the Institute!' Once there I'd strike up a conversation with the locals and have a few drinks with them. Rum and ginger was the popular drink in the 50's, or beer if it was really hot and humid.

I was an instant success in Gestetner! By April, only

three months in my position as Sales and Service Representative, I was picking up commission cheques worth ten times my monthly salary! For the first time in my life I had money in my wallet to spend as I liked. This is when I met my wife-to-be!

Jean Ford was a 'girl from the country'. She was gorgeous! Slim, long legs up to her armpits and a wonderful sight in a red-and-white candy-striped dress when I first set eyes on her! It was love at first sight. Within two years we were married and she has been the love of my life for the last 49 years. Along came our first son, Dean, born at the end of 1953 in Agra, the city of the famous Taj Mahal.

A year later I was transferred to our Calcutta branch. As a Sales and Service Representative I worked a senior territory handling nearly all the large European commercial customers on the famous Chowringhee strip.

Well, I was back in my old hometown again! I renewed my acquaintance with my married-again father, who was a Calcutta Rangers Club member. He supported my application to join this prestigious Anglo-Indian club and I played hockey and soccer for them for ten years.

In 1955 I was promoted to the post of Supervisor of Gestetner's Entally plant, set up in Calcutta to manufacture Gestetner machines and supplies for the Indian market. I reported to an English Works Manager whose name was Roy Tamplin. A nicer bloke one could not find. During those eventful years in Calcutta I was sent on a three-month training trip to the English factory at Tottenham, London. On my return to India I was made officially the Assistant Works Manager. In 1960 Roy was needed to start up a factory in Argentina along the same lines as the Indian factory, and I was promoted to Works Manager of the Entally plant. I did this job diligently till we emigrated to Australia in 1964.

During our ten years in Calcutta my wife Jean had

presented me with three more sons: Floyd, Paul and Barry. So with a wife and four boys, I ventured forth to a new land to start a new life in Australia.

The last months in India were nerve-wracking. The Indian Government with its red tape was a nightmare for people travelling overseas. Passports, Reserve Bank Clearances and airline tickets were all such a headache that we often wondered if we would ever get out of the country! At last, though, with all formalities completed, we left Dum Dum airport in Calcutta on a flight to Bangkok. After a night's stopover there we went on to Hong Kong. The kids were completely fascinated with television in both Bangkok and Hong Kong, as we had no television in India back in 1964. Then, finally, we were on the flight to Sydney, Australia via Manila in the Philippines.

CHAPTER TWO: Dhyan Chand to Charlesworth–An Overview

Field hockey, as it is known in most British Commonwealth countries, was my favourite sport from a very young age, say about seven years old.

My earliest recollection is playing in teams of about four or five in the street. The street was Theatre Road, now called Shakespeare Serani, in a suburb called Park Circus in that huge city of Calcutta, in India. The year was 1938. The traffic was not heavy – very few motor vehicles but plenty of horse-drawn phaetons (called gharries in Hindi) and a few rickshaws, pulled manually by the humble rickshaw-wallah, or man who pulled rickshaws for a living. The occasional bullock-cart slowly rattled past.

Our frantic game of street hockey was tough, no-nonsense stuff, with plenty of bruised shins and other abrasions. We loved it! We played some days for hours on end! When one of us would duck off to have a bite to eat the game just carried on with those left behind. The surface of our 'hockey field' was coal tar or tarmacadam. Two house-bricks acted as our 'goals', about fifty yards apart. The slightly raised pavements (curbs) on either side of the road were the side boundaries. It was 'out' if the ball went up on the pavement! If it bounced off the curb and back onto the tarmac it was 'play on'! Some evenings we played till well past dusk until 'light stopped play' or our parents insisted we come indoors.

When I was sent, at the age of eight, to boarding school, my street-playing days and 'experience' stood me in good stead. I already knew how to handle a hockey stick and was thus one of the better players around.

In the schools I attended – St. Thomas' in Calcutta, St. Michael's in Patna, St. Edward's in Simla and finally St. Joseph's College in Naini Tal, in the Himalayan Mountains – precious little coaching, as such, was encountered. We were 'organised', yes, but never 'coached' in the finer points of the game or its skills for the ten years that I was a boarder at these schools.

In the hill schools (St. Edward's, Simla and St. Joseph's, Naini Tal) the grounds we played on were very bumpy, as the surface was usually *'budgeree'* or small pebbles. Trapping was a nightmare to those who did not practice very hard, but the diligent ones were rewarded when they returned from school and played at home on well-grassed surfaces. It was a 'snack' trapping the ball on a good surface! It gave one so much more time to 'look up' or 'scan' before passing the ball.

THE CRADLES OF INDIAN HOCKEY

Not many Indians played hockey at a competitive level before the Great War (1914–1918.) The game was popular in railway colonies in which Anglo-Indians predominated, the Services, some vernacular schools in Punjab and Bombay, and in the Anglo-Indian and European schools such as the ones I attended. It was there that the youth of British India acquired the background that enabled them, when they grew older, to go on and win Olympic Gold Medals for India in 1928, 1932, 1936, 1948 and 1952. By the end of the British Raj in 1947, there were enough good players and clubs to sustain the sport for a further ten years at top level, to 1956.

The 1956 Melbourne Games marked the end of the Anglo-Indian era. They had carried India to six Gold

Medals on the trot. By 1960 (Rome) there was only one Anglo-Indian left in the Indian National team, attending his fourth Olympiad – hockey legend Leslie Claudius, the captain. Pakistan beat India there and started an era which lasted twenty years.

India won again, beating Pakistan in the 1964 Tokyo Olympic Final, and also won the World Cup in 1975 in Kuala Lumpur and the Gold Medal at the Moscow games in 1980. However, the Moscow Games were boycotted by the strong hockey nations.

Since then India has not done too well. Pakistan has also steadily declined as a hockey power. It was tragic and almost unbelievable to see India play Pakistan to decide *last* place at the London World Cup in 1986. What a complete turn-around!

The situation has been quite the opposite in the emerging hockey nations, like Australia (World Cup winners in 1986) and New Zealand (Olympic Gold winners in 1976). It is no wonder that, from the eighties these countries have become a force to be reckoned with in field hockey. Together with traditionally strong European nations like Germany, Holland and England they have laid strong emphasis on dedication, physical fitness and playing on synthetic surfaces. They have also reaped the benefit of strong indoor hockey competitions, utilising skills learned at indoor hockey (like flicking, horizontal trapping, etc.) to their advantage on outdoor synthetic surfaces. Lastly, Australia and New Zealand in particular have had the supreme benefit of a steady influx of Anglo-Indians with the schooling and hockey background that I share.

Back to the early days of my life! In the thirties and forties school hockey was played either at 'Inter-House' level or 'Inter-Class' level on an organized basis. The Inter-Class competitions were held between the 8th, 9th, 10th year and college sections. Inter-school matches were also organized, and the town 'open' tournament was played too. All in all, a college or school First XI shirt was much prized.

Hockey season in the hills was usually between March and May, before the monsoons broke and rain washed out play. Soccer took over in late May and ran till the end of August, as soccer could be played in the 'wet'. Athletics came next, followed by cricket. Tennis and rowing had separate sections and went on all the year around.

In the college I last attended, St Joseph's in Naini Tal, run by the Irish Christian Brothers, First XI boys were even given special treatment in the dining room. We got 'toasted' bread, along with the 'Parlour' Boarders or 'Privileged' kids, while the rest got un-toasted bread. I might add that this was considered a real privilege and a treat!

When we boarders got home for our holidays we usually joined a local club and learned technique, tactics and ball control, along with positional play. A lot of lads came from railway 'colonies' and towns like Kharagpur, Bilaspur, Asansol in the East and Lahore, Ajmir, Rawalpindi in the North, Bombay, Bhopal, Nagpur in the West and Centre, and Bangalore, Madras and other towns in the South of India. This was where the good hockey of any note was being played in those early years.

Calcutta, with the largest population of domiciled Europeans and Anglo-Indians, had a powerful Club League. Legendary teams like the Calcutta Rangers, Calcutta Customs, Bengal Nagpur Railways, Licensed Measurers, Port Commissioners, Mohun Bagan, Mohammedan Sporting and in more recent years East Bengal dominated the games. Crowds of up to ten thousand were quite common at a top game. The ladies with their parasols (umbrellas), the men with their Panama hats and 'solar topees' (pith hats) graced the occasion. A band usually played at half time and good-natured barracking and much laughter could be heard. My early memories of a good game included a lot of clapping and laughter. In fact it was so good I was intoxicated with the atmosphere. I wanted to play this game, more than any other, when I grew up!

At the age of seventeen I went to live in London, England, and got a job through a friend in that large travel conglomerate Thomas Cook & Sons, in their head office close to Berkeley Square, in Central London. On weekends a group of us who hailed from India met in London's Hyde Park and had an impromptu game of hockey. I looked forward to those sunny Sundays and our 'free for all' games with very few rules.

ENGLAND

I remember particularly a set of brothers named the Beards. One was called Arnie and the older one was Les. Les played centre half-back and Arnie centre-forward. They hailed from Allahabad in Uttar Pradesh and had been educated in a town called Muree in present-day Pakistan. We got a few guys together and because Les worked for the Indian High Commission in London we played as the 'Indian High Commission XI'.

The hockey Gold at the London Olympiad in 1948 was won by India with Anglo-Indian players Pat Jansen, Gerry Glacken, Leslie Claudius and some excellent Goan players Walter D'Sousa, Leo Pinto, Laurie Fernandes and Reggie Rodrigues. Sikh players Balbir Singh, Trilochan and Dharam Singh starred with outstanding Punjabi Hindu players Amir Kumar, Keshav Dutt, and from the UP, the legendary K. D. Singh (Babu) and the captain, Kishen Lall.

Pakistan had a player called Latif Ur-Rehman who played left-wing in London; he stayed on in London after the Olympics to further his studies. Latif played in a 'friendly' against our team for the Pakistan High Commission. We (the Indian High Commission XI) won that match with every single player in our side an Anglo-Indian. I played right-half that match, with Les Beard at centre-half.

The 'Pakkies' could not believe their eyes! Here was a bunch of 'whites' beating them at their National sport. All our guys were products of Anglo-Indian boarding schools in India where we had played from about the age of nine. I'd say Latif-Ur-Rehman, if he should read this, may recall the game well because he 'never got a hit' as the saying goes! The year was 1949.

At the end of 1949 I returned to live in India, as I hated the cold and wet of post-war, coupon-wielding, ration-conscious London. I had enjoyed the jazz and soccer (I was a Chelsea supporter) but really wanted to return to India.

DELHI

In 1949 the Indian National Championships were held in New Delhi at the Lady Harding ground near the Rivoli Cinema at the back of Connaught Circus, now called Shivaji Stadium. I went to the games, eager to see some of the greats in action.

Bengal had Rex Peters in goal, and in my opinion the fullbacks were ordinary (D. Pal and D. Bannerjee). Claudius was great to watch. Gerry Glacken at centre-forward was a 'hit-and-run' player and not, in my opinion, up to Olympic class. He was reserve centre-forward to Balbir Singh in the London Games. Punjab won the National Championships that year in New Delhi, with Balbir, Udham, Ragbir Lal, Dharam and Tilrochan Singh as the full-backs and Sahib Singh the centre-half. Daido Maish and the others made it a great side!

I started looking for a job in New Delhi in January 1950. During the day I went job-hunting, but in the evenings I practised my hockey skills on the balcony of our flat in

Connaught Place. For a couple of hours a day I'd be playing with stick and ball, until one day a neighbour in the flat above who had been watching me with interest and amazement at my dexterity with hockey stick and ball suggested I join a local club. He had a friend who attended Delhi University and played with a club called the Delhi Independents. Their home ground was adjacent to Rajghat, the spot where the great Indian leader Mahatma Gandhi was cremated. It was a 30 to 40 minute ride on a pushbike from Connaught Place, in the very hot afternoon sun, but I was keen to play so I fronted up.

From the start I realised it was not going to be easy, as I was the only Anglo-Indian there! When I approached the man who was apparently the organizer of the practice game, one Mehtab Narain, he was most helpful and encouraging. Mehtab spoke beautiful English and was a fine player and coach. He had a simple philosophy. 'If you are dedicated to the sport, diligent in your endeavours, listen and practice, you must be better than the next guy who does not have these attributes!' In me he felt he had an 18 year old who had good basic skills of hitting, trapping and dribbling and who was wiling to 'put in' to become a good player.

Delhi Independents' Club team-mates that come to mind are: Lala Kasturi Lall; Vishnu Narain, a bespectacled classy forward who later went to Calcutta to play with the renowned 'Babu' in the Bhowanipore Hockey Club; and R. S. Gentle, who was a fellow-member before he went to Bombay to star with the Tata Sports Club and eventually play full-back for the Indian Olympic team. Our right-half was K. L. Sethi, the brilliant State player. An ex-great in pre-Partition days was Sikander Bakht, a wonderful hockey supporter and coach.

The Delhi Independents were to Delhi hockey in the 40's and 50's what the Cricketers Hockey Club was to Perth hockey in Western Australia. Here was a club rich in tradition and bristling with hockey talent. Legendary Delhi State player in 1942, Sikander Bakht and three-time Olympic Gold medal winner R. S. Gentle were from this club. Kasturi Lall, Sethi, Noble (Gentle's brother), Feroze, Nauroze, Autar Singh, Bipen and best of all Mehtab Narain himself, were my team-mates, along with Inder Lall, a fierce full-back, and bespectacled Vishnu, a super inside-forward with great stick work.

Gentle later went to Tatas (Bombay), the then National Airline and Steel Conglomerate. Vishnu went to Calcutta and played for a club called Bhowanipur, a First Division side in the Calcutta League.

Being in the top hockey club had its 'downside'. I played at right-half but was in the second team with an older guy, Noble, (R. S. Gentle's brother) as centre-half and captain. I stuck with it, rather than join another club to play 'firsts' but with no hockey advancement. Playing four seasons in the second team of this top club – 1950, 1951, 1952 and 1953 – I learned my hockey well, mainly from Mehtab Narain.

In 1951 a group of us Delhi Anglo-Indians got together and played socially in an invitation tournament at the Roshenara Club in Old Delhi. From memory there were Glen Montgomery, Fred Long, Gerry Miles, myself, the Harding brothers, Don Hoffland and Roger Milchem. We played under the name of the 'UK High Commissioners X1' and won the tournament. We had an enjoyable and great win!

Feeling pretty good about ourselves we travelled to a town called Dehra Dun, at the foot of the Himalayas, to play the NDA (National Defence Academy). This was India's equivalent of Australia's Duntroon. It was the military academy where the nation's talented and privileged were made into Officers and Gentlemen. They were too good and far too fit for us and though the score was 2-2 at half time it finished up 7-2 in their favour. Their best player was a Maurice Britto, who went on to represent his state, Bombay, at the Nationals when he left the Army.

One of the top hockey and football (soccer) umpires in Delhi at the time was Gian Singh. As a hockey umpire he went on to officiate at two Olympiads and later became the hockey coach of Thailand and also, later still, Singapore. Gian was a prolific writer of hockey books, some of which were translated into Russian. Usually writing manuals on umpiring or coaching, he also wrote hockey quiz books on the rules of the game. Gian travelled to Montreal and wrote a book on the tournament in 1976 which is a classic record of all the matches on the new Astroturf surface, called *Olympic Hockey, on Astroturf*.

While with Delhi Independents hockey club I went on a couple of hockey trips out of town. The first was to a country town called Bullundshar in the then United Provinces (this was a state adjacent to Delhi). The dusty, hot trip in a crammed bus for three hours was a trial of endurance. We played in a local knockout tournament on a hard smooth mud surface. The ball moved lightning fast but I never missed a trap all day, playing at right-half. Unfortunately we lost 1-0 to the local police team, which made the spectators happy. It was my first taste of truly competitive hockey and I loved it!

The trip back was enjoyable with heaps of singing! I could not join in as the lads (all Indians) were singing in their local dialect Punjabi, which I could understand but certainly not sing in! Most enjoyable and whetted my appetite for more hockey trips away.

The next trip was to the famous Indian Mutiny town called Lucknow, which was 300 miles east of Delhi. This time the train was our method of transport. Third class was the 'go', costing very little, which suited nearly all the players who were either students, unemployed or in small low-paid jobs. Crowded in like cattle, my vivid memory was of a horror night. If it hadn't been for the excellent company and our mutual love of hockey it would have been much worse.

Again we met a local Police Garrison team. Very fit guys, but we held our own till our opponents scored, late in a close game, to win 1-0.

These knockout tournaments are really tough. One loss and you are on the way home. *'Gharrie Pukro!'* was the crowd chant towards the dying stages of the game! That means in translation 'Catch the train'! I loved going on these trips, despite the train rides, the poor accommodation and food. The mere companionship and hockey was what we cared about – nothing else! No complaints – just roll the sleeves up and get on with the game!

You may recall my mentioning earlier that in April 1950 I joined the English firm Gestetner Ltd. As a Gestetner salesman attached to the New Delhi branch I often went on extended field trips. While on a field trip I remember playing for the Moradabad Institute (East India Railway) Team with the legendary Anglo-Indian Jimmy Lemmondine. He must have been forty-five then, and I was around twenty-one, but we combined together and we enjoyed our game The two Lemmondine brothers were hockey legends in those parts during the thirties and forties. I feel privileged that I played alongside Jimmy. He was old, short and bald, with a hockey stick that looked 'out of the ark', but could he play hockey! He was a master of dribbling and made us younger guys feel sick with envy, admiring his stick skills.

I am forever grateful for my early hockey experiences in New Delhi and for the lasting friendships I made. Nearly forty years later I revisited Delhi and caught up with a lot of my 'Independents' mates. Some of them had reached pinnacles of success. Yogeswar Dayal was now a wealthy businessman, my old coach Mehtab Narain was a Doctor of Psychology, and Sethi – the guy who kept me out of the right-half spot in the first team – was now a junior coach. Kasturi Lal, now retired, owned a motor scooter and insisted I ride on the back of it while he took me to meet old friends like Sikander Bakht, now a Senior Party Official in the Federal Government in New Delhi, and ex-Olympic captain of the Gold Medal team in the London Olympiad, Kishen Lal. I was flattered to hear Kishen Lal say to me, 'I remember playing against your team, the Rangers Club in Calcutta, in the Beighton Cup in the fifties.' Kishen Lal was by then playing inside-right for Western Railways, a team with several great players – players like Erman, Ashlyn Saxby (now living in Perth, Western Australia) and centre-half Joe Antic are some of the names that come to mind.

One evening after training, about sixteen of us went to Sikander Bakht's home in the nearby suburb of Darya Gunj to listen to him 'talk hockey'. We sat on the floor at the feet of a man who knew his subject. He was also a very successful person outside of hockey; in fact he was a political organizer when I visited him years later (1978) on a trip to India from Australia with a West Australian team.

Listening to Sikander was a joy for me. That night at Sikander's place I knew without a doubt that I wanted be a hockey coach one day, and impart my knowledge of the game as he had done: clearly, precisely, logically. He sounded so sure of himself and his knowledge of tactics, positioning and mental preparation. This was the mark of a great coach!

And so my four-year 'apprenticeship' with the second team of the Independents Hockey Club ended on a marvellous note, with the crystallisation of my own ambitions. Those years, 1950 to 1953, left me with great memories and many good friends. But I cannot leave the Delhi scene without a mention of other hockey players who were my contemporaries.

A few years earlier the Anglo-Indians in New Delhi had formed a team called the Hornets. I never played with or against them but did hear of their better players. Names bandied around were Casi Ticklo, Gerry Miles, Don and Verni Hoffland, Ray Harding, Fred Long, Glen Montgomery and Mervin Gaynor. I did see Montgomery later when he played in a team called the Khalsa Blues. Glen was a fine centre-forward with dash, stick work and heaps of skill. Gerry Miles was also 'a natural', having made his mark in tennis, badminton and soccer as well as hockey; a true all-rounder remembered by many to this day in New Delhi.

Gerry emigrated to Perth in the late 60's and took up golf, dying of a heart attack in the late 70's.

CALCUTTA

When I got transferred in my job to Calcutta I promptly joined the famous Calcutta Rangers Club. This club was the bastion of Anglo-Indian sports in Calcutta. In the late 1800's they were known as the 'Naval Volunteers'. To be a member one had to be an Anglo-Indian. Hindus, Muslims, Goans and Indian Christians could not join, and Englishmen had their own clubs. In the period right up to the War – in fact, even till 1942 – the top sides in Calcutta hockey were: Rangers, Customs, B.N.R. (Bengal Nagpur Railways), Port Commissioners and Measurers. Hindus played for Mohun Bagan, Greer Sporting and Aryans, Muslims played for Mohammedan Sporting, and Armenians for the Armenian Sports Club.

The two major hockey events in Calcutta were the League, where all sides in First Division played each other twice, and the Open Invitation Tournament, the All-India Blue Riband of hockey, the Beighton Cup, named after an

Englishman who was the Remembrancer of Bengal in 1895.

The Rangers Club had seen better days in hockey! They were still in First Division but struggling, as nearly all the talented Anglo-Indians had been 'poached' by rich Indian clubs to play for incentives or had left the country. The 'good' or talented players still with the club were Fred Gormanly, Horace Rodrigues, Albert Holder, Trevor Blake and a youngster called Charles Crizzle. After these six the standard fell away badly so I was welcomed when I joined. The first season that I was there, 1954, we played quite well and Rodrigues, Crizzle and Holder went on to play State hockey for Bengal. One of India's finest players at the time, the legendary Leslie Claudius (two gold medals at the time, went on to win three Olympic Gold and one Silver!), captained Calcutta Customs, who also boasted players like Gurbux Singh (captained India in 1968), Dougie Gardner, who was in school with me in Simla, Rudy Pacheco, who grew up with me in New Delhi and now lives in Melbourne, Haripada Guha (State), Dalgeet Singh (State) are some names that come to mind from those early days. Dalgeet moved to Bombay and was tragically murdered.

Most local clubs in Calcutta held their team selection meetings on a Thursday, for the game on Saturday or Sunday. The Rangers team 'book' was filled in with the team selections and positions and also had the 'reserves' listed. On Thursday evening the club would send the book to each player's home for him to 'sign' his availability or otherwise with the words 'yes' or 'no'. The book told him where the game was, the bully-off (starting time), the opponents and who else had been selected. Last-minute arrangements had to be made on Friday in case someone was unavailable due to illness or any other reason. A regular excuse was 'going to a wedding'. I was one who just loved to play and no excuse ever came from my lips – or pencil, when the book came to me.

I played ten seasons with the Calcutta Rangers Club and six as captain and ad-hoc coach, since in India then the captain usually coached the team as well.

Not only was I player/captain/coach of the Rangers' hockey team, but I played football (soccer) for the Club as well, and considered it a privilege to play. I did not need persuasion. At one stage in 1957 I was so fit I felt I could play a second game the same day!

Then there was the 'Mussellwhite Cup' for the Commercial Office Team Competition. My firm Gestetner (I was factory Assistant Manager at the time) allowed me to employ who I liked in order to field a strong team! I did, and we won the Cup in our second attempt. We beat a team called Blackwood Hodge in the final. Office League standard was not very high, and I had the nucleus of the Rangers' First Division team working in our factory, and getting them to play for the firm was a condition of employment as it were! We were too strong for the other office sides so we withdrew after a few years.

THE BEIGHTON CUP

As I have mentioned before, this was the 'Blue Riband' of Indian hockey tournaments held in Calcutta every year since 1895, and named after an English officer, a Mr. Beighton, to commemorate his contribution to Bengal hockey. Teams travelled hundreds of miles to participate in this prestigious tournament. They came from Bombay in the west (Tatas, Western Railway, Central Railways), Punjab in the north (Punjab Police), Madras and Bangalore in the deep south (M. & S.M Railways, Hindustan Aircraft and Corp of Engineers), from Bhopal (Bhopal Wanderers), UP (K. D. 'Babu' Singh's team UP X1), Kharagpur (BNR), Asansol (Burnpore United) and many other centres. Some of the very best hockey in the world at the time was witnessed on the famous Calcutta Football Club (C.F.C.) ground. The ground secretary, a man by the name of Georgiadi, kept the C.F.C. surface like a bowling green. It was an absolute joy to play hockey on it. Perhaps because it was so level top players hardly ever missed a trap on it!

My biggest thrill was when I was skippering Calcutta Rangers in the Beighton and we played Western Railways, captained by ex-Olympic captain Kishen Lall, It was a great effort by my team to hold this seeded team to a 1-2 loss. We really had them worried. They had a team of champions like Antic, Erman and Saxby, but we nearly toppled them on that occasion Best of us on the day were Trevor Blake, Albert Holder (later played for the USA), Charlie Crizzle and Horace Rodrigues. Fred Gormanly and I played inside-forward, very defensive. Kishen Lal who was playing inside-right was marking me as I lined up as inside-left for our side. When they hit the front 2-1 late in the game Kishen Lall was heard quite clearly yelling at his players to play for time, to start hitting the ball 'out'.

Another time, due to the fact the outstanding team in our half of the draw withdrew late from the tournament, we got into the semi-final and had to play the crack military outfit called 'the Corps of Engineers'. They boasted a giant of a full-back who played for India, a player of great strength named Murthi. Their inside-right was also an Indian International called Peter. Peter was his surname (he was an Indian Christian). Fantastic stick work but, in my opinion, a bit timid! Anyway, they took it easy on us and cruised to a 4-0 win, scoring two goals in each half. The Corps of Engineers went on to lose to Mohun Bagan in the final on a controversial umpiring decision which soured the win. Mohun Bagan had the great Keshav Dutt (Gold 1948 and 1952), Piara Singh, David and Wahi-Dullah playing for them. From memory, the following year the two teams met again in the final, and the result was reversed.

'SHAMATEURS' AND PROS

There was a core of 'pro' players playing for incentives delivered under the counter (unofficially), as it would otherwise hinder their chances to represent India at the Olympics if proof were available that they were not amateurs but 'pros'. Because the Anglo-Indian 'pros' Rodrigues, the Baker brothers, Thompson, the Holder brothers, Conwell, Peters and others all held low-paid jobs they left the 'lily white' Rangers to play for incentives being offered by the rich Hindu and Muslim clubs, who needed them to boost their chances of winning the Calcutta league.

In 1957 I persuaded our club (Rangers) committee to agree to offer incentives to some of these 'shamateurs' with a view to enticing them back to play for us. Horace Rodrigues and Eddie Conwell used our offer to get a better deal from their Indian friends, but others did come back to play for us.

The Rangers team then comprised Rex Peters (ex-State) in goal, Rudy Baker (ex- Mohd Sporting) and Reggie Peters full-backs, Albert Holder (played for Bengal State and for the USA later), myself (Vanderputt) centre-half, Trevor Blake left-half, Crizzle (later played State), Fred Gormanly, Desmond Holder, Eustace Thompson (ex-Mohd Sporting) and Terry Vears, a *kackie-hand* (left-hander!) on the left wing.

We did really well that year, finishing behind the big four: Mohun Bagan, East Bengal, Mohd Sporting and Customs. To come fifth out of seventeen teams was a good effort, especially since we sacked Rex Peters midway through the season for excessive demands beyond the agreed incentives and dates!

Some memorable games were played that season, but it was the Rangers' last real shot at glory on the Calcutta hockey field. Farley Baker came in at left-half and Trevor

Blake and Reggie Peters shared the full-back spots. Farley who went on to play State hockey in 1959 was a very sound, solid left-half who gave his opposite number barely 'a touch'. He went on to live in the UK and played hockey there with an old school buddy of mine called Norman Marley. Albert Holder took off for the USA via the UK without so much as signing 'no' in the team availability book.

Some other Anglo-Indians who played at that time at top level were: 'Bunny' Thompson (Mohun Bagan), Eddie Conwell (East Bengal), Sydney Edge (Measurers), Pat Doyle (Dalhousie Athletic) and 'old-timers' Pat Jansen (Dalhousie Athletic), Karl Grueber, Henry Strong (Rangers), Merv D'Sousa, Stan Mullick and Alan Gardner (Police), Cox (Aryans) and Len Smith, (Chakradharpur), Noel Sutton (Burnpore United), Leon Lee (Hyderabad), Ashlyn Saxby (Bombay), Nigel Richtor (Madras), McBride, Archer and Fitzgerald (Hindustan Aircraft Factory Bangalore), Jimmy Carr (Madras Railways) and Mervyn Gaynor (Delhi).

The list goes on and on. I do hope some of these guys get to read this book some day and feel that they were remembered as great players who took India to the top of the hockey tree.

ON SPORTSMANSHIP

One afternoon on the Rangers Club ground our team, the Rangers, were playing a dull match against another equally-low placed team, the Aryans, the result of which did not matter very much to either team. I hit a ball close to the back line of the opponents' goal and the ball went in via a hole in the side of the netting. The referee awarded what he thought was a 'legit' goal. The opponents loudly remonstrated but seemed to be getting nowhere with the ref. I knew, of course, that it was not a goal so I went up to the ref and said, 'No goal, ref, it went in from the side'. He promptly awarded a 25-yard Bully, which was in force in those days. We went on to win 2 or 3 nil anyway, but that little bit of sportsmanship was blown up next day in the 'Statesman', the prestigious English daily newspaper.

One sees little of this sort of thing these days! Maybe the current 'win at all costs' attitude has robbed the game of pleasantries such as 'good sportsmanship' and 'playing the game'.

STATE SELECTOR, BENGAL

The Bengal Hockey Association appointed me as State Selector in 1959. Other selectors that year were Keshav Dutt and team manager/coach Balbir Kapoor. In this illustrious company I helped pick a squad for the Nationals. Youngsters Crizzle, Holder and Eustace Thompson were selected along with stalwarts Farley Baker, Horace Rodrigues, Eddie Conwell and Leslie Claudius. Seven out of 18 players were, Anglo-Indians, which was a huge slice of the team. That year Bengal won the title at the C.F.C ground in Calcutta. Claudius went on to skipper India at the Rome games in 1960. India lost to Pakistan 0-1 in the final and India's iron grip on the Olympic Gold (five in a row) was at last brought to an end, ironically with only one Anglo-Indian, the captain Leslie Claudius, in the side.

ANGLO-INDIANS ABROAD

At those Games Anglo-Indian players who starred for Great Britain were Freddy Scott and John Conroy; and for Australia, the Pearce brothers Julian, Gordon and Eric, and also Kevin Carton. It was the end of an era for Indian hockey and the start of the rise of Australian and British hockey at this level.

At the next Games (Tokyo1964) Australia, under

Queenslander John McBride (now living in Canada), won their first Olympic hockey medal, a bronze, beating Spain for third place. Then in 1968 (Mexico), with what many thought was Australia's best side, including Pat Nilan, Ron Riley, Brian Glencross and the Pearce Brothers, Don Martin and Don Smart, the Aussies lost a rough game in the final to Pakistan and thus won the silver.

After a lapse due to team rebuilding, the Australian team, now under Arthur Sturgess as coach in Munich (1972) missed the 'cut' and finished fifth! Under new coach Merv Adams they lost in the Final in 1976 (Montreal), this time to New Zealand. In 1980 when the Australian team was at its peak, the political boycott of the Moscow Olympics kept Australia out, and they lost a golden opportunity.

Then came four years of unprecedented success! Winning the Champions Trophy, the Peugeot Cup, in Europe they failed disastrously in Los Angeles in 1984, losing quite unexpectedly to Australia's old nemesis Pakistan in the semi-final.

After licking their wounds and going back to square one and rebuilding the team, the Aussie performance in Seoul was nevertheless again surprisingly disappointing. Everyone in hockey circles had expected Australia to win an Olympic Gold in 1984 and again in 1988, but defeats at crucial times shattered coach Richard Aggiss and Australia's dreams. The forwards were not up to it when the pressure was on!

Again back to the drawing board! New coach, Aggiss's protégé, Frank Murray a student of the game and an astute coach, planned the 1992 Aussie assault on 'Gold' in Barcelona. His forwards would have to improve and mature if Australia were to win the big one (Gold.)

In Frank Murray Australia thought they had the right man for the job. He ignored reputations and played most times the form and fit players, something his old mentor Merv Adams had taught him. Merv coached both Frank

Murray and Richard Aggiss in the Modernians Hockey Club in the early seventies.

History shows, however, that Murray did not succeed where Aggiss, Adams, Sturgess and Morley had also 'failed', in not winning an Olympic Gold Medal. That is, if coming second or third could be called 'failure'!

THE RISE AND FALL OF INDIAN HOCKEY

After Anglo-Indians and Goans (people of Portuguese descent), arguably the best players in India were Punjabi Muslims, Punjabi Hindus and the Sikhs. With the end of the British Raj, most Anglo-Indians moved on to Australia, the UK, Canada and New Zealand. Many Muslims migrated to the newly-formed Pakistan which left the Sikhs as the hockey power in India in the 50's and 60's. Gian was a Sikh and proud of it but regrettably, seldom fully acknowledged Muslim or Anglo-Indian greats of the game in any of his numerous books.

To hockey lovers, Sikhs were good, physically strong athletes and the record shows how they dominated for twenty years. However, unlike the Muslims in Pakistan in the 60's and 70's their administration was, sadly, found wanting. Ashwini Kumar did a lot for Punjab and Indian hockey but he favoured the Punjabis and the game thus suffered in the traditionally strong hockey centres of Bombay, Bengal, Madras and Bangalore. Only teams belonging to the Services, Police, Railways and Airlines (Tatas and IAC) were able to offer employment all over the country to budding hockey players. Hockey died in centres like Ajmer, Delhi, Lucknow, Bhopal, Kharagpur, Madras and Bangalore. Many schools stopped playing hockey once the Anglo-Indians left India in the late forties and fifties. With no juniors coming through and poor administration, the game took third preference to cricket and soccer. Many people outside India still mistakenly think hockey is India's national sport – not so! The petty interstate rivalries, the constant 'feathering of nests' and 'pushing one's own barrow' was the bane of Indian hockey. Good people would not come forward to 'work' for the game! They preferred to further their own careers and sadly, the people left to run things failed miserably. The results at top hockey levels prove this!

No new initiatives were put forward for years on end, and when people of the calibre of Pankaj Gupta, Sidhu Dutta, Ashwini Kumar and Gian Singh lost favour or died, hockey reached the depths in which it now finds itself in India. A proud tradition of over sixty years had gone down the drain between 1960 and today, where India finds it hard to field a team to beat Canada. I ask you – Canada? Ice Hockey, yes – but not Field Hockey! (I say this with due respect to John McBride.) Teams like Australia, the Netherlands and Germany could give India a four-goal start now and still win on most occasions, a far cry from the 20's, 30's and 40's. The slide started in the 50's, and consequently India lost the Gold Medal in 1960 in Rome to Pakistan.

ALL-TIME HOCKEY HEROES INDIA

'MISTER HOCKEY'

India's 'Mr. Hockey' was a Bengali named Pankaj Gupta who simultaneously administered both the Bengal Hockey Association and the Indian National Hockey Federation (IHF) for nearly forty years. Pankaj was a good friend of mine and I served with him on both BHA (Bengal Hockey Association) and IFA (Indian Football Association) Councils in the fifties.

Pankaj was the master at organizing and fund raising. He also served athletics, table-tennis and a host of other sports, but his first love was hockey. In his early years Pankaj was an international umpire who always managed the travelling Indian hockey teams.

Pankaj loved a drop of whiskey and enjoyed telling us stories of hockey and its characters over the many years that he was at the helm. Pankaj had his detractors, but no one could deny his contribution to hockey in its heyday in world circles. He was not easily put off and showed things could be done if only people got off their butts and got on with the job. The Beighton cup was Pankaj Gupta's pride and joy.

Teams from all over India were invited, their train fares paid and money provided for their food while at the tournament. A massive job of organization! In addition, Pankaj Gupta wrote the articles for the Souvenir Programme, looked after the VIP guests, ordered the trophies and did the thousand and one things that we now have numerous committees to take care of. Pankaj Gupta, son of Bengal and India's great hockey ambassador for decades when India ruled the hockey world like a colossus, was awarded the coveted British MBE (Member of the British Empire). I too, in my own small way, wish to pay high tribute to this great man who loved hockey and worked so hard for it.

LESLIE CLAUDIUS

'Youngker', as we called Claudius (because he always looked so young!) was a superb centre-half for his club and his State but played right-half for his country. He never seemed to 'tackle', invariably intercepting and passing to a player. I never saw him ever miss a trap either! And remember those were days on natural grass, not Astroturf or Poligrass.

Cool under pressure, Claudius would often come out of the goal when all seemed lost and pull the ball off the goal line! '*Eh ta* (Bengali 'This is') *Claudius!*' or '*Hail Claudius!*' was the awed cry of praise, making him sound like a victorious Roman Senator when he pulled off an impossible save or made a super measured well-balanced (weighted) pass that split a defence.

One of hockey's all-time great players, who dominated the hockey scene for 25 years, Claudius starred in four Olympiads, winning three gold and one silver. He was slightly built, unlike his brothers Erroll and Derek, but superbly fit, and he read the play beautifully.

Leslie Claudius, who hailed from a small country town called Bilaspur on the old Bengal Nagpur Railway (B.N.R.) joined the Calcutta Port Commissioners and played with such greats as Pat Jansen (Gold 1948), Balbir Kapur and Joe Gallibardy. Claudius moved later to the famous Customs where he played First Division for over twenty years with great distinction, representing the State of Bengal for seventeen seasons and captaining the side ten times – a truly remarkable record, hard to equal or even come anywhere near!

Claudius started playing Internationals in the late forties and ended in the late sixties. He also coached and managed Indian International teams and acted as a Selector, a marvellous contribution, acknowledged by the President of India.

INDIAN HOCKEY 'GREATS'

In summary, the super 'true-blue' Indians indelibly etched on my mind as hockey greats are:

'Wizard' Dhyan Chand
Roop Singh, Dhyan's brother
Amir Kumar,
Perumal
Ragbir Lal
Balbir and Udham Singh

Ramswaroop
Sahib Singh
Bakshish Singh
Jaman Lal Sharma
Keshav Dutt
Purshottam
Amir Kumar
Uni Krishen
K. Aurora
K. D. Singh (Babu)
Add Anglo-Indians of old like:
Penniger
Mead
Nyss
Norris
Minto
Brendish
Allen
The Davidson brothers
Hodges
Claude Defolts
Robin Neil
Percy Damzen
Carmen (later played for Pakistan)
Dique
Cullen
Woodcock
Frank Wells.
These were all great players.

If I had to pick a best-ever Indian team of twenty from my own years of experience as player and selector, and also after listening to old-timers, it would be something like this:

Goal:
ALLEN (Bengal)
Reserve: SHANKAR LAKSHMAN (Services)

Backs:
TAPSELL (Bengal)' GENTLE (Bombay)
Reserve: Ivan MEAD (B N Railway)

Half Backs:
Right   Centre
CLAUDIUS (Bengal) PENNIGER (Punjab)
GALLIBARDY (Bengal)

Reserves:
Keshav DUTT (Punjab/Bengal)   Amir KUMAR (Punjab/Bombay)

Forwards:

Right Wing	*Right Inside*	*Centre*	*Left Inside*	*Left Wing*
Dick CARR	BABU★	Dhyan CHAND	UDHAM	BHOLA
(Bengal)	(U.P.)	(Army)	(Punjab)	(Air Force)

Reserves:
Kishen LALL (Bombay); Roop Singh (UP); Balbir SINGH (Punjab);
Pat JANSEN (Bengal); RAJAGOPAL (Mysore)

★Babu was awarded the prestigious Helm's trophy by US journalists as the most complete and brilliant sportsman at the Helsinki games (1952).

ANGLO-INDIAN PLAYERS IN OLYMPIC TEAMS
INDIAN TEAMS

1928	Allen, Rocque, Hammond, Norris, Penniger, Gateley, Marthins, Seaman, Cullen
1932	Allen, Tapsell, Hammond, Penniger, Carr, Brewin, Hind
1936	Allen, Tapsell, Cullen, Gallibardy, Emmett, Mitchie
1948	Jansen, Claudius, Glacken
1952	Claudius, DaLuz
1956	Claudius
1960	Claudius

AUSTRALIAN TEAMS

This list includes sons of former Anglo-Indian players.

1956	M. Pearce, G. Pearce, E. Pearce, Carton, Kemp, Browne (Coach)
1960	G. Pearce, E. Pearce, J. Pearce, Carton
1964	Watters, J. Pearce, E. Pearce, Smart
1968	J. Pearce, E. Pearce, G. Pearce, Smart
1972	Smart
1976	Walsh, Poole, Adams (Coach)

ENGLAND TEAMS

Fred Scott, John Conroy, Jon Potter.

PLAYERS WHO PLAYED MULTIPLE OLYMPICS

FOUR OLYMPICS	THREE OLYMPICS
India: Leslie Claudius, Udham Singh★★ *Australia*: Eric Pearce, Ric Charlesworth★★	*India*: Richard Allen★, Dhyan Chand★, Balbir Singh, Shankar Lakshman *Australia:* Don Smart, GordonPearce, Julian Pearce, Brian Glencross, Ron Riley★, R. Haigh, Pat Nilan, Ray Evans, Des Piper, Paul Dearing

*Richard Allen and Dhyan Chand would have played four Olympics had World War II not intervened.

*Ron Riley would have played four Olympics but for the Moscow boycott.

**Udham Singh would have played five Olympics had he not injured his hand just prior to the 1948 Olympics, and Ric Charlesworth would have played five Olympics had Australia participated in the Moscow Games.

NOTED ANGLO-INDIAN COACHES

India:

Rex Norris Holland, Italy, Spain in the 1940's and 1950's. As a player, he won Olympic Gold in 1928.

Australia:

Dennis Dunbar St. Pauls, Darjeeling; Adelaide and Perth. Suburban H.C. and University Of Western Australia Hockey Club in the 1930's.

Fred Browne La Martinere College, Lucknow. Selected as Australian Olympic coach 1956.

Cyril Carton Western Australia State senior coach, 1950's.

Dick Carr BNR Kharagpur Olympian Gold medal 1932, Sydney St. George H.C. 1950's.

Merve Adams La Martinere College, Lucknow; Perth Western Australia Senior Coach 1960's to 1970's and men's Olympic Coach 1976 (won Silver Medal.)

Derek Munrowd, Gren Davis, Pearce Brothers, Don Smart all contributed to advancing the standard of Australian Hockey at State or Australian level.

CHAPTER THREE: INDIAN HOCKEY

The Irish Christian Brothers and Anglican schools, through their educational institutions, and the British Army were responsible for bringing the game of hockey into the Anglo-Indian community of India. Consequently several Anglo-Indian players were selected for the first Olympics in which British India participated in 1928. In the next Olympiad (1932) a few Muslim players started to make their presence felt. By the 1936 games there were six Muslims in the team and one Sikh. Then a small village in the Punjab by the name of Sansarpur started a tradition for producing Sikh players of renown. Their tough and skilful playing combined with astute coaching saw the Sikhs produce three players of quality, selected in the National team for the 1948 London Olympics. By 1952 there were five Sikhs in the national team. The Sikhs of Punjab State also produced a team called the Punjab Police that won nearly all the major tournaments throughout the length and breadth of India. Some say this was due to the loss of Muslim players by the formation of Pakistan and also to the mass migration of the Anglo-Indians from India to Australia, New Zealand, Canada and Great Britain. Whatever the reason, it could not be denied that the Sikhs were now the dominant force in Indian Hockey, in the 50's and 60's.

THE SIKHS

This community hails from the land of the five rivers, Punjab. They are easily recognizable by their headgear (Pugrees), facial hair (beards) and strongly-built physiques.

Coming from the North, they are a tough and handsome breed of people. They traditionally make very good farmers, truck drivers and mechanics. Most of all they are noted for their fighting qualities and, along with India's other fighters the Rajputs, figured prominently in the wars with the invading Muslims and British in past Indian history. This fighting quality carried into their love of many a manly pursuit, one of which was the noble game of hockey.

Sikh players that stand out from the records are: Gurmit, Gurcharan, Trilochan, Grahanandan, Balbir, Udham, Dharam, Gurdav, Balkrishan, Amit, Hardayal, Prithipal, Joginder, Charanjit, Jaswant, Gurbux, Harbinder, Darshan, Jagit, Ajitpal, Inder, Gurbaksh, Balbir (1), Balbir (2), Balbir (3), Mukhbain, Harmik, Kulwant, Harcharan, Verinder, Baldev, Mohinder. Most of these were International players during a period when India was the team to beat in World Hockey.

Five Gold Olympic medals and a World Cup was the wonderful result of a magnificent contribution by the Sikh Community and their fellow Punjabis like Swami Jagan Nath, G. D. Sondhi, Kehar Singh and Feroz Khan; Lal Shah Bokhari, Aslam, Jaffar, Hind, Masud Minhas and Dara; M. L. Kapur, Keshav, Amir Kumar, Ram Prakash, Ram Sarup, S.M. Yousif, Ragbir Lall and Harbail Singh (Olympic Coach in 1952 and 1956, also an accomplished International Umpire); Professor Gursewak Singh, Gursawak Singh Mela, Kishan Lall and Kulwant Aurora.

The greatest off-field contribution, however, was from Ashwini Kumar, the then Deputy Inspector-General of Police, and later President of the Indian Hockey Federation. His encouragement of Punjabi players, whether they were Sikh, Hindu or Muslim, was the driving force of hockey in the 50's and 60's.

Another famous Sikh contributor was Delhi's Sardar Gian Singh. This man has written books on hockey that have sold throughout the hockey world in various languages. He has held Coaching positions in Thailand and Singapore, umpired at the 1956 Melbourne Olympics, and has been to Internationals all over the globe. I personally know he has been to Montreal, Perth, and Kuala Lumpur, and is one of India's great hockey ambassadors. This doyen of hockey for over forty years was also a first-class soccer referee.

OTHER PUNJABI AND HINDU PLAYERS

Some other observations and opinions formed by the Author during those years on other Punjabi and Hindu players and administrators:

PANKAJ GUPTA

I call this man from Bengal 'Mr Hockey' of India! From the start of India's participation on the International scene Pankaj was the driving force. He ran the Blue Riband hockey tourney in Calcutta called the Beighton Cup on the immaculate bowling-green type surface of the Calcutta Football Club. Teams were invited to participate from all parts of India. Army teams, Railway teams, Company teams, leading Club teams, and even State teams all loved to come to Calcutta to play with the best players in the world. It was strictly a knock-out tourney: one loss and you were out. When a visiting team was seen to be losing, the happy Bengali crowd would ironically chant '*Garrie Puckroe*' which means 'Catch the train!'

Pankaj was an International hockey umpire and blew at the 1932 Olympics. He was manager of numerous teams that went abroad in those years, besides being involved with sports other than hockey, including football (soccer), and athletics.

In 1932, and again in 1936, the Indian Olympic

Committee was finding it impossible to procure funding to send our hockey team to the Olympics. Both times Pankaj used his persuasive powers to get the famous Calcutta Rangers Club, which was a Club that ran the Calcutta Rangers Sweepstakes four times a year and thus were very rich in funds, to support the hockey team with a large donation, thus enabling the players to travel abroad.

Many hockey fans and supporters do not know that they have Pankaj Gupta and the Calcutta Rangers Club to thank for this sponsorship, without which world hockey history would have missed India's massive and skilful contribution to the world game.

Other well known Sikh and Punjabi Players of India were as follows:

Piara	Pershorie Lall	Dalgeet
Kulwant Aurora	Dadoo Maish	Ram Swaroop
Raghbir Lall	Manna	Balbir Kapoor
Surgit	Pargat	

Hindu and Indian Christian players were also prominent in Indian Hockey's halcyon days. Some that spring to my mind are as follows:

Haripada Guha	Bhansode	Balloo
T. Shah	Unikrishan	Mohinder Lall
Antic	Erman	R.S. Bholla
Shankar Lakshman	E. Manual	V. Deshmukh
Jhaman Lall Sharma	Gurung	Tikken
Arthur	David	R.S. Gentle & Nobel
Bandoo Patel	Perumal	Rajagopal
Suraj Balram	Veer Chand	K.L. Sethi
Lalla Kasturi Lall	Mehtab Narain	Vishnu
Ranga Das	Kothanda Pani	

Goan Players that shone in this era were as follows:

| Walter D'Sousa | James D'Costa | Sacru Menezies |
| Maurice Britto | Joe Dennis | Venicio Carvalho |

Joe D'Sousa   Joe D'Mello   Leo Pinto

Muslim Players of note were:

Shaukat Ali	Arif	M.Naeem
M. Rahaman	Sultan Khan	Nazir
Mustaq Ahmed	Munir	Quddus
G. Rasool	Wahidulla	Anwar Ahmed
Aktha Ali	Hamid	Asid Ali
Mohamed Ghouse	Jakir Din	

Anglo-Indian Players who were the greats of yesteryear:

F.C. Wells	C. Tapsell	R.J. Allen	R.J. Carr
C. Hodges	P. Jansen	P.A. Da Luz	T. Mendies
L. Claudius	C. Deefholts	O. Broodie	E. Ford
S. Minto	J. Robson	S. Penniger	D. Byrne
C. Dique	H. Brendish	R. Neil	C. Smith
B. Joost,	Vears	F. Seaman	D. Jardine
Weston	M. Smith	W. Cotton	R.G. MacInnes
E. Martin	J. Renton	G. Nyss	N. Scott
W. Scott	P. Damzen	M. Gallarbady	J. Gallibardy
C. Rebello	I. Meade	A. Alexander	R. Joost
R.F. Scott	P. Archard	Johannes	L. Davidson
W. Davidson	C. Harbin	R. Roche	P. Symes
Mitchie	E. Durham	Turnbull	Sweeney
G. Glacken	E. Nestor	L. Tapsell	Emmett
T. D'Sena	R. Peters	T. Mendies	C. Andrews
Z. Carapiat	S. Edge	H. Rodrigues	F. Baker
R. Baker	H. Thompson	E. Conwell	C. Crizzle
F. Gormanly	L. Lee	Huggins	M. Gaynor
Macbride	Archer	Fitzgerald	G. Montgomery
M. Petters	A. Holder	A. Saxby	P. O'Hallorin
N. Richtor	L. Cotter	J. Carr	R. Lefaucher
J. Lemondine			

Hockey enthusiasts reading this book will be puzzled by my omission of a number of prominent players, including the

53

greatest name of all: Dhyan Chand. This is because the next section is devoted to outstanding Indian players, beginning, of course, with Dhyan Chand.

HOCKEY PERSONALITIES–INDIA

DHYAN 'THE WIZARD' CHAND

The name conjures up memories of Indian hockey's Golden era. Known in Europe after the 1928 and 1936 Olympics as the 'Wizard' for his dazzling stick-work, passing skills and goal shooting, also his tactical brain in hockey and general demeanour on a hockey field, Dhyan Chand was a match-winner of renown, along with his brother Roop Singh.

Dhyan was born on August 29, 1905 in the Uttar Pradesh town of Jhansi. If he were alive today (2002) he would have been 97. He passed on to that great hockey field in the sky on December 3, 1979 at the grand old age (for an Indian) of 74.

In 1928, still unknown to the top echelon of players and selectors, Dhyan represented United Provinces during the Inter-Provincial Championships, helping to lift the title with his wizardry. This display earned him selection for the 1928 Olympics at Amsterdam where he won his first Olympic Gold Medal. He went on to be an automatic selection for the next two Olympics, where he collected a further two Gold Medals. If World War Two had not caused the cancellation of the 1940 Olympics he would undoubtedly have won a fourth Olympic Gold Medal.

Dhyan had a burning desire in his youth to train and bring a team to Calcutta that could win the top tournament, the Beighton Cup. In 1934 he had his wish come true.

Playing for his beloved hometown team, the Jhansi Heroes, alongside his brother Roop Singh and a fast-running brilliant winger Ismail, this intrepid leader took on and beat the best teams of the era at the Beighton Cup in Calcutta in 1934.

In a memorable Final the Jhansi Heroes, with Dhyan leading them, beat Calcutta Customs 1-0. It was Ismail the winger who scored the winning goal off a through pass from the master Dhyan. Customs had some great players in their side that day, including Shaukat Ali, Asad Ali, Claude Deefholts, Seaman and Mohsin.

The team's train trip back to Jhansi in a crowded third-class compartment, to be met by a huge turnout of local hockey fans and others, was always a wonderful memory for the great Dhyan Chand, hockey player extraordinaire.

People I have spoken with over fifty years always spoke of his brilliance both as a player and a captain of the team. I was privileged to see him play in an exhibition match just before he retired. The game was on the famous CFC ground in Calcutta. Dhyan was by then 45 years old, with a heavily strapped left knee, but in spite of his years and some very tight marking he took control of a cross pass from his left wing at the top of the opponents' circle and in a flash the ball was in the net, a feat which to this day is fresh in my mind.

The Indian Army gave their star sportsman much support and Dhyan progressed from Lance Naik (Corporal) to the officer corps, first as Captain, then as Major.

The Internet quoted Dhyan referring to himself as a 'common man' as he lay dying in hospital. This he was not! Dhyan Chand, the Wizard, was truly 'The Greatest!' As a player he was completely unselfish. His ball-skills and ball-passing to a team-mate were a treat to watch. His final shot on goal was deadly accurate. Players that played inside-left to him (Roop Singh was one) were often served goal-scoring opportunities on a platter.

When I visited Kuala Lumpur in Malaysia in 1975 to witness the World Cup, Dhyan's son Ashok Kumar scored the winning goal in the Final against Pakistan to win the World Cup. Dhyan would have been pleased if he were there to see his son carry his name forward. Other stars that day in my opinion were Coach Bodi, Ajitpal Singh and left winger Harcharan Singh. Seventy to eighty thousand spectators in the Merdeka Stadium gave the Indian team a standing ovation and *I was proud to be from India!*

ZAVEN 'BULBUL' CARAPIAT

ARMENIAN HOCKEY CLUB AND BENGAL

When I first set eyes on this player on a hockey field what I saw was an extremely fit, strong running player who had an unorthodox (left-handed) grip and could flick or scoop a hockey ball over fifty yards at will. He was most effective on wet grass or when his team was under immense pressure. Working from, say, near his own circle he could flick fifty yards to his right wing beyond the opponents' twenty-five. He was so effective that he was selected in the Bengal team to play in the National Championships to be held in Madras in 1951. A local journalist from the 'Sport and Pastime' newspaper, one Surendra Rajan, had the following to say of Bul Bul:

Speaking of personalities, I am reminded of the doings of Carapiat (Bengal), he of the unorthodox grip fame. As one writer put it, chasing Carapiat was like attempting to catch a cat in a room full of furniture! He was very elusive and his shoves and scoops cleared a lot of ground.

That year Punjab, with a very strong team, beat Bengal after three wonderful matches that saw scores of 0-0, 2-2, and 2-1. Punjab went on to beat the Services team 1-0 in the Final.

The following year, 1952, was Bengal's year of triumph. The Nationals were held in Bengal and the Bengal team, led by Dick Da Luz (Capt.) with Tom Mendies in goals, and Les Claudius, Pat Jansen, Z. Carapiat, C.S. Gurung and Haripada Guha beat Services in the Semi-Final and came up against the then Champion team Punjab in the Final. With Pat Jansen injured the selectors in their wisdom chose Bul Bul to replace him. The Punjab team was uncomfortable playing against this player who had caused such havoc against them the previous year in Madras. Carapiat played the game of his life and was responsible for his team holding the great Punjab team to 1-1. In the replayed final, Jansen was brought back into the Bengal side and it won a memorable game 2-1, much to the delight of the fully packed Bengali crowd. The Sikhs were still shocked and could not get over the run-around Carapiat had given them the day before.

Carapiat also played soccer and cricket for my Club, the Calcutta Rangers. A truly great all round sportsman, he also starred in rugby and is remembered to this day in Calcutta. He emigrated to Australia and lives in Dee Why, a suburb of Sydney. At the time of writing this (2001) he is well and is now 72 years of age.

GURBUX SINGH

MOHUN BAGAN HOCKEY CLUB & CUSTOMS H.C.
BENGAL AND INDIA

This stalwart hockey full-back was first spotted as a potential great player in his academic years at Aligarh University in the state of Uttar Pradesh. Like a moth attracted to a flame, Gurbux arrived in Calcutta to further his hockey dreams. His father started a motor spare parts business, which catered for a huge motor industry in which Sikhs were very prominent as taxi and truck drivers. The business thrived and so did Gurbux's role as a good hockey player.

Playing most of his early hockey life in Calcutta for the

Calcutta Customs as right full-back behind the 'Master' Leslie Claudius, Gurbux was soon recognized as a sound defender and was selected in the Bengal team in 1957, 1958, 1959, and then continuously for many years into the 1960's culminating in being selected for the 1968 Mexico Olympic team as Captain.

The author played against Gurbux on numerous occasions between 1955 and 1960 and was always impressed with his demeanour on the field: scrupulously fair and a person of complete integrity both as a team man and a person off the field as well. Gurbux in his later years played for the mighty Mohun Bagan Club where he won Premierships and a Beighton Medal as well. He was selected as India's National Coach for the Montreal Olympics in 1976. India had started to fade as an effective force in international hockey. Gurbux had been Captain when they lost to Australia in Mexico and again when he was Coach in 1976 in Montreal. In 1980 Gurbux was made an Indian selector and his team won back the Olympic Gold Medal in Moscow.

In 1978, the author took a team comprising mainly Perth players from the Cricketers Hockey Club on a tour of India. Then 40 years old, Gurbux captained Mohun Bagan with Ves Paes at centre-half and Ashok Kumar (son of legendary Dhyan Chand) playing inside-right. Cricketers were led by Australian legend Ric Charlesworth, with a heavily strapped right thigh. Charlie showed Calcutta fans what a good player he was – even on one leg! The tussle was on: Gurbux, one of India's best ever against Charlesworth, one of Australia's best. The author, who managed the Cricketers team that trip had to admire his old friend, who at 40 was opposed to the finest inside-right of the day and still came up 'Best on Ground'. The Aussies won 2-1 but Gurbux was really outstanding in spite of his team losing.

The author has visited Calcutta, the city of his birth, on

several occasions and always calls on his old friend Gurbux Singh.

One last memory: Like the author, Gurbux wore spectacles while playing. The only other Indian players who played at this level and wore spectacles while playing were Alan MacBride (Hindustan Aircraft, Bangalore) and Vishnu Narain (Delhi Independents and latterly Bhowanipore H.C. Calcutta), the old team-mate of K.D. Singh, the legendary 'Babu'.

The highest Indian Award for achievement in sport, the prestigious Arjuna Award, was bestowed on this great Indian hockey player, coach, captain, selector and finally President of the Bengal Hockey Association. Well done, Gurbux Singh! You have made a great contribution to hockey!

LT. COLONEL JOHN FONSECA, VSM

SERVICES COMMANDANT, ARMY SCHOOL OF PHYSICAL TRAINING

John Fonseca was well known in Sporting Circles as he was in charge of the Armed Services Boxing and Hockey teams in the sixties. His best hockey team was the one that represented the Services in 1965. In that side he had five Indian Internationals. Peter, Manual and Shankar Lakshman were the stars. The giant of a full-back Murthy was a pillar of strength. The author remembers playing against Murthy when he represented the Corps of Engineers in the Beighton Cup.

Summarised are some of the highlights of a busy sporting career:

BOXING:

Won the light middle-weight title in 1942.

Manager/Coach of the Indian Boxing team to South East Asian Boxing Championships.

Indian Coach to the Cardiff Commonwealth Games, and the Rome Olympics.

FOOTBALL (SOCCER):

Played for the Services team in an International Match against Ceylon in 1950.

HOCKEY:

Captained the Eastern Command team.

Indian National Umpire from 1957.

ATHLETICS:

Coached and accompanied Indian Athletic teams abroad.

Visited Germany as an International Starter at Frankfurt and Munich and was invited to the 1972 Olympics by the German Athletic Association.

GYMNASTICS:

Coach/Manager of the Indian Gymnastics team that toured USSR in 1963.

From this brief commentary one can see the mighty contribution Lt Colonel Fonseca has made to Indian hockey and in fact all sports – a great and unparalleled effort that deserves the highest praise. Lt Col. Fonseca, now retired and living in Perth, Western Australia, has fond memories of his charges in the Indian Services teams both in hockey and boxing. Fonseca excelled in sports administration and contributed to many Indian sporting achievements.

PATRICK 'PAT' JANSEN

PORT COMMISSIONERS / BENGAL / INDIA

Pat was born in Bangalore in South India and went to school in St. Joseph's College, Bangalore. He moved to Calcutta and was soon recruited by the Calcutta Port Commissioners who had a very strong hockey team.

Pat came into prominence as a goal-scoring inside-left when his team won the League and Beighton Cup in 1946. They then won the League again in 1948 and Pat was selected to represent India at the London Olympics. He played in all matches and scored a goal in the Final in India's 4-1 Gold Medal win. The star for India that game was right-winger Kishan Lall, who kept putting in some wonderful cross-passes from the right. K. D. Singh (Babu) was inside-right and Pat was left-inner to Balbir Singh. Bombay's Laurie Fernandes was the speedy left-wing to Pat. The half-back line was Keshav, Amir Kumar, and Maxi Vaz, who had a wonderful understanding with his fellow Bombay mate Laurie Fernandes. Trilocan Singh and R. S. Gentle, the former Delhi Independents player, now with Tata Sports, were the backs and yet another Bombayite, Leo Pinto in goals. The British team never had a hope of beating this Indian team of Champions.

On his return to Calcutta Pat was hailed as a hero and awarded the Bengal Captaincy. He was picked to tour East Africa (Kenya) with the National team which included an aging Dhyan Chand, Babu, Keshav, Gerry Glacken, and Balbir Kapoor, a centre-half from Pat's own Port Commissioners team in Calcutta. The tour was a great success.

Pat was a hard-working inside forward who, with a turn of his wrists, could completely hoodwink a defender with beautiful passes to his other players in the forward line. His famous flick from outside his left side scored many a brilliant goal.

Pat emigrated to Australia in the late 50's and helped the author when asked to speak to the West Australian under-16 State side at a training match. He was very impressed with Peter Haselhurst, who was only 15 at the time, and agreed with the author's predictions of great things for this brilliant young forward. Peter, of course, went on to partner the great Ric Charlesworth in the Cricketers Hockey Club and took part in the 1978 tour of India. He played later for the State (WA) sides and the Australian National teams of the late 70's and early 80's.

Pat, playing for India, had to wear a traditional Pugree for the March Pasts and ceremonial occasions and was sometimes unrecognisable as an Anglo-Indian, but he was proud to wear the Indian Pugree and wore it with distinction (see photo). He was, of course, carrying on the tradition of fellow great Anglo-Indians who represented India, the land of their birth (Penneger, Allen, Tapsell, Claudius and so many others.) Well done, Pat Jansen, and thanks for the memories!

25TH NOVEMBER 2001

> The Author has just heard the sad news of the death of ex-Anglo-Indian Olympian (1948 London Games). Pat Jansen, who was 80 years young, had suffered a stroke some time back but was still playing social Veteran's tennis, when he collapsed on the tennis court and died instantly on 23 November 2001. My condolences to his wife Joan and his family. Elsewhere in this book there is more on Patrick Jansen.
>
> Pat Jansen, Rest in Peace!

MERV ADAMS
BOMBAY/WEST AUSTRALIA/AUSTRALIAN NATIONAL COACH

This great Anglo-Indian was born in India in 1920 and was educated at Christ Church Boys High School, Jubalpur, and then later attended the famous La Martiniere College at Lucknow, one of the most ancient of India's great cities.

It was at 'La Mart' that Adams learned his hockey, under the coach Fred Browne, who was later to become the first Australian Olympic Coach at Melbourne in 1956.

La Martiniere College was to be the setting for one of the great moments in the life of Merv Adams. Here he came under the spell of the great 'Indian Wizard' Dhyan Chand, considered the greatest hockey player of all time, and Captain of India in the 1936 Berlin Olympics. After a match against a school team captained by Adams, the Wizard commented that 'here was a player with a very bright future.'

Merv built a career in the Bombay City Police and rose to the rank of Deputy Inspector in 1947. It was in this year that he made the decision to emigrate to Australia.

Merv's Australian career is covered in the chapter headed 'Western Australia'.

JOE GALLIBARDY
B.N.R., PORT COMMISSIONERS, BENGAL, INDIA

The little Indian railway colony known as the cradle of Anglo-Indian hockey was a town called Kharagpur on the then Bengal Nagpur Railway. Being a large railway centre with a large Anglo-Indian and domiciled European community, the hockey teams that came out of Kharagpur in the 30's and 40's were truly talented hockey teams.

World-renowned players like Carl Tapsell, Richard Carr

and Joe Gallibardy (all won gold medals at the pre-World War Two Olympic Games.) Tapsell was the first full-back to make a name for himself in scoring from penalty (short) corners, with awesome hitting power. Richard Carr (better known as Dicky Carr) was famous for his wizardry with hockey stick skills in the forward line. Equally at home at centre-forward, right-inner or right-wing, Dick emigrated to Sydney, Australia, in the late forties and played for the St George Hockey Club. One of his protégés was Brian Booth who played test cricket and later Olympic hockey for Australia. Richard Carr was remembered by New South Wales greats such as Kenny and Harry Wark, Victor Westcott and Ivan Spedding, players that were in awe of his game while he was in his late thirties. Carl Tapsell settled in Queensland.

I never saw Dick Carr or Carl Tapsell play but know a lot of people who did and their records speak for themselves. I did see their mate Joe Gallibardy who was still playing First Division in Calcutta in his late thirties when I was in my early twenties. Joe was a superb left half-back. He is famous for inventing a few tactics. He was supposedly the first player to 'push out' on penalty corners. Most grounds were so poor that nothing but a hefty hit would carry the ball to the top of the circle. Kharagpur, where Joe played his early hockey, had a superbly kept, smooth grassed hockey field, and Joe and his BNR (Bengal Napur Railway) team mates started experimenting with a quick push which disguised the moment of impact that a hit would signal. Carl Tapsell would then carry the ball inside the circle a couple of yards and blast it in with monotonous ease.

Joe's other claim to hockey fame was his 'roll in' (by hand in those days!) from the side line. He perfected hand and stick signals to his team mates and made possession from a roll in an easy set play. Many times he would make a large swinging action but leave the ball on or near the line and move off and allow his team mate to run in and take possession! The rules were later altered to prevent this manoeuvre during 'roll ins'!

Joe played close to his sideline and in his zone. Seldom did he allow his winger to get a 'through pass'. He wanted his opponent winger, if at all, to collect the ball 'square' and 'in front' of him. This was his contribution to tactical left half play. He was up behind his forwards and would, when in possession, sometimes dash into the forward line and have a shot at goal. He was so quick and had such good control he was able to do this much to the disgust of his coaches. Many a time he was threatened that if he continued on these 'sorties' he would be 'dropped' from the team. ' His job was to 'feed the ball to his forwards' not take off with it and run the risk of being dispossessed and leave his 'opposing player' unmarked.

Joe recalled that in Berlin in 1936 for the Olympics the German team coach and manager met the Indian Team the night they arrived at their hotel and asked if they would like to have a 'practice game' with a 'club' side next day. This friendly practice game was welcomed by the Indian Team after a long sea journey from India via London. The ground was a 'paddock' and a quagmire with the recent heavy rain. The Indians wore their sand shoes (in India no one wore boots or footwear with studs or spikes for hockey as the grounds were traditionally hard and fast!), not only could they not run too well, they could hardly keep on their feet. The 'club' side turned out to be the German Olympic Team 'in disguise' and they handed the unsuspecting and, as far as footwear was concerned, ill-equipped Indian Team a 4-1 drubbing on the eve of the Olympic Tournament.

The Indian management then decided that they needed another 'class' inside-right because Dick Carr could not make the trip. An 'SOS' went out and Dara (later to play Olympic hockey for Pakistan) was hurriedly sent out to join the team.

The tournament went as expected, with the tournament favourites for the 'Gold', Germany, playing at home in front of their Leader, Adolf Hitler, with the memory of the 4-1 drubbing and with their morale high, the 'Gerries' got the shock of their lives in the final! The Indians now had proper footwear and with Dara at inside-right, Dhyan Chand at centre-forward and Roop (his brother) at inside-left, Jaffar on the right wing, a half line with Gallibardy and Cullen, with Tapsell and Hussain fullbacks, and with incomparable Richard Allen in goal, the Indians blasted the hapless Germans 8-1 to win India's third Gold Medal, having previously won in 1928 & 1932. The goal India conceded in the final was the only goal they conceded in the entire tournament!

Another legend from the Bengal Nagpur Railway's great team of the forties was Ivan 'Honey' Meade. He played fullback with Tapsell. Ivan migrated to Perth in the late forties, and coached at the Perth YMCA Club. There was a photo of the YMCA U/16 Junior Boys Team with Ivan Meade the coach hanging in the Club rooms. In their 1960 side were Brian Glencross and Don Smart also. Brian went on to captain Australia and win a Silver Medal at the Mexico Olympics as a player, and a Gold at Seoul as the Australian Women's Coach. Don Smart went on to three Olympics, winning Silver and Bronze, and was one of Australia's great players with dazzling stick skills! I have never read or heard anyone giving 'Honey' Meade any credit for coaching the great Brian Glencross or Don Smart in their formative years.

Joe Gallibardy migrated to the UK and finally settled in Spain. On a holiday visit to Australia in 1991 I had the pleasure of meeting him and took him out to our Commonwealth Hockey Stadium in Perth. He was very impressed with the facility and watched three games of the

Classic League with interest. As an old left-half he could not fathom why modern day left half-backs chase 'their' winger to the opposite side of the ground when he takes off! I explained this was the way modern coaches trained their players but he, like me, remained puzzled. 'What happened to 'zone hockey'?' This 'man-to-man' was more like Australian Rules football, not hockey!

I asked him what his greatest disappointment was. He felt that it was missing out on playing for India in the 1948 London Olympics, when he was at his peak, in his opinion, and could have been selected. He had had to withdraw due to family pressure. His wife was having one of his seven kids and his mother-in-law put her foot down! His greatest moment? When he stood on the Olympic dais to collect his Olympic Gold Medal. I then asked about the great Dhyan Chand and learnt from Joe that even though Dhyan scored heaps of goals he was a most unselfish player, and wonderful team man. He never spoke to umpires and always loved the game.

This love of the game runs like a thread of gold through a tapestry of all the truly great players. Pat Nilan of Sydney, Des Piper of Melbourne, Barry Dancer of Queensland, Mike Nobbs of Adelaide, Colin Batch of Victoria, the Pearce Brothers of WA, and of course the best of all, in my opinion, Richard Charlesworth of Australia. Coaches Merv Adams, Brian Glencross, Richard Aggis and Frank Murray all loved the game; this is why they were and are successful. The message, if there is one, to hockey players or coaches is –*love the game!* It will reward you in return with heaps of enjoyment in this modern world of pressures and turmoil.

CHAPTER FOUR: SYDNEY, AUSTRALIA 1964

My family and I arrived in Australia as migrants from India in July 1964. The sensational British pop group The Beatles had arrived in Australia the week before us. Their music was playing on nearly every radio, and the top tune of the week was It's Been a Hard Day's Night. We rented a place in Manly on the road adjacent to the famous beach, in a block of old-fashioned units called Dungowan. The currency was pounds, shillings and pence, and a 'middie' of beer cost under two shillings.

It was really obvious from the start that we needed some form of transport, as with a wife and four small kids it would be both inconvenient and expensive catching public transport for work or entertainment. We bought a Volkswagen Model 1500 sedan, having read previously that the VW 1200 was most reliable. I figured the new model 1500 would have to be both better looking than the Beetle, and more up-to-date as far as features were concerned. On reflection, this was the first big mistake I made in a new country. The new car would not start on cold winter mornings. After quite a few visits to the car dealer who had sold us this 'bargain' to try and rectify this annoying defect I decided to sell the car in spite of losing money after such a short time being the owner of a brand new vehicle. I then bought a Holden.

First impressions! Coming from India there were a few things that took getting used to here in Australia. Everything we noticed we couldn't help comparing straight away to what we had experienced in Calcutta as a young family.

We had never owned a washing machine in India as we had Dhobies (laundrymen) who collected all the dirty clothes and household linen once a week. These they took away to launder and iron for a pittance. We had never had to prepare or cook our meals, or even make our own cup of tea, as servants were relatively inexpensive in Calcutta at the time. Then came the general household cleaning chores. We had had jamadars or sweepers to do this. Suddenly my wife had a load of heavy work to do herself, and the days of being the memsahib had suddenly come to a stop. All these normal household chores seemed to come so naturally to Aussie homemakers and European migrants, but to our wives it was a really tough assignment.

Even shopping for groceries was an entirely new experience! A visit to the local butcher had been a rare venture, as our cook in India always did this job. Our food had always been cooked with a clarified lard called 'Dalda' in India, and we had taken its perennial presence in the kitchen for granted. Now we had to explore the fascinating world of cooking mediums for ourselves! Knowing that 'Dalda' was an Indian brand name unheard of in Australia we asked for 'ghee' but met with blank stares. We settled for olive oil.

The next stop was the green grocer. We asked for 'brinjals'. 'Never heard of them!' came the reply. It turned out we were after eggplant. 'Ladies' Fingers' were okra!

After all this shopping I needed a new purse. I went into a men's clothing store and asked for one. The looks I got were priceless!

'It's a wallet you want, mate!' I was informed gruffly. 'Purses are for ladies!'

Well, how about school stockings for the boys?

'No, mate. Only women wear stockings. They need school socks!'

'We also need night suits,' I said timidly, afraid of the response.

'Really! That's pyjamas, mate!'

This list of different names for the day-to-day things we required goes on and on. I won't bore you any more with it, dear reader, but it should bring back vivid memories for many migrants who share our background.

I had worked for an English company called Gestetner in India for fourteen years. When they heard I was migrating to Australia, the Head Office in London wrote to their Australian subsidiary and asked them to employ me on my arrival in this country.

We had arrived Sydney on a Friday. First thing on Saturday morning I caught the Manly ferry and after a wonderful cruise on the delightful harbour, I caught a bus out to Rushcutters' Bay, the suburb where Gestetner had its offices. To my utter shock the whole place was locked up! I asked a local why it was closed, he reminded me that it was Saturday! What a relief! For one horrible moment there, I thought I was in a strange country without a job! I had not realised that most offices closed on Saturdays as we were accustomed to working half days on Saturdays in Calcutta.

Come Monday morning all was well. After a very brief interview I was shown a huge map of Sydney and its environs and my 'territory' was explained to me. I was to start work as a Supply Sales rep on Gestetner supply products and if I proved I could cope, I could sell duplicating machines as well, later on. To me this was no problem. I had been a successful machine and supply rep in India for five years before I had been promoted to the Manufacturing side of the business where I remained till I emigrated to Australia. I was allocated a company car to use between the hours of 9 and 5. Les Hearne, one of the Head Office staff, got to use the same car after work hours. This was fine by me as I had my own car for after hours. It was just the way the company operated, to save money.

The work was a piece of cake for me and I got stuck in right from the start. Not knowing my way around Sydney in the early days I would pick up Jean, my wife, and she would sit on the front seat beside me with the street directory in her lap and direct me to the customers. My Supply/Service Manager John White was a wonderful person who assisted me in every way once he realised that I was experienced and not a complete beginner, and I could do the job without supervision.

And so, very quickly, the home and work fronts were organised.

Now for my other great love – Hockey!

A popular local newspaper, The Sydney Morning Herald, advertised that a hockey match was to be played at Jubilee Park playing field that weekend. I looked up my street directory and found there was more than one ground under this heading. I chose one of them at random, on the other side of town from Manly where I lived. It was a 45-minute drive across the famous Sydney Harbour Bridge and past the airport. When I got there I found it to be a small recreation park and obviously not a hockey field. I then raced back to the other Jubilee Oval, which was in a city suburb called Glebe, and thankfully was much closer to my home.

The match of the round was St. George Hockey Club versus the Glebe Hockey Club, then the top two sides in the Sydney competition. The game had started some fifteen minutes earlier, and I took up a spectator's position behind the Glebe goalpost. The standard of hockey was reasonable. After watching for a while I asked a fellow spectator who were the stars in the teams.

Pat Nilan was the first name to be mentioned. Pat was a

Glebe player who was then the National team's inside forward. He was really a treat to watch. Slim, very fit, wonderful stick-work and passing skills, topped off with a fine shot on goal. A well-balanced hockey player!

On the Saints' side my companion mentioned Brian Booth, a very well known Test Cricketer, who had represented Australia in both Test Cricket and International Hockey. He, too, was a fine player, though getting on by this time. This fellow spectator standing by my side was very friendly and obviously a Glebe supporter. He asked me what my name was. I told him.

'Vanderputt!' he exclaimed. 'What do you know! This Glebe goalkeeper of ours – his name is Frank Vanderputt and comes from your neck of the woods.'

It turned out that Frank was from Ceylon (now Sri Lanka) and born of parents of Dutch descent like myself. In Ceylon they are called Burgers and in India they are called Anglo-Indians.

After the game I decided that Glebe was the club for me. They trained on Wednesdays, and their ground was only a short drive from my work, so it suited me.

Pat Nilan was the skipper of Glebe's First Division squad and Fred Letts was the President. Frank Vanderputt was the Secretary. All three made me feel really welcome on joining. After a few weeks at club training I was included into the Second Division team. The skipper of the team was one of the two famous Glebe players, Harry Wark.

I was 33 years old and had stopped playing First Division hockey in Calcutta some three years previously. I was therefore delighted to hear that hockey in Australia could be played even though one was past one's best and getting on in years. Here they held competitions for Second, Third and Fourth Division grades for the same club in addition to the First Division tournaments.

I soon learned that the club had a great hockey tradition. Formed in the low socio-economic suburb of Glebe they grew them tough, and thus we had tough no-nonsense hockey players. Some called them too rough! I thought them great blokes and wonderful competitors. Some of the great Glebe players and friends I either trained with or played with in Second grade were the Howes, the Wark brothers, Gillie (Gilmore), Vic Westacott, Paul Rodgers, Lennie Needham, the Lisks, Peter Krepp, Russ Nicholls, Bennet Dunn, Don Barker, Bill Stubbs and Robert (Charlie) Brown. Wonderful guys! All of them loved hockey and were solid drinkers, and our clubhouse often rang to the sounds of our merriment.

Our clubhouse was just as unique and picturesque as the club itself. It was called Under the Arches because it was an old viaduct with two of the arches enclosed. Our second 'home' was the popular Tokteth Hotel, a drinking hole in Glebe Point Road frequented by the local 'wharfies', a really tough looking mob – though other clubs in the League might have thought the Glebe Hockey players were tougher!

Whilst in Sydney, the Pakistan (Olympic Titleholders at the time, they won this in 1960) were on a Pre-Olympic Tour on their way to Tokyo to defend their title in the 1964 Olympics. The Australian Team was pretty strong back then in 1964. From memory the team was: Paul Dearing in goal, McCormick and Glencross backs, Julian Pearce centre half, Gordon Pearce right half. Forwards were Robin Hodder, Ray Evans, Eric Pearce, Pat Nilan (Piper was injured) and G. Wood, was left wing.

The Pakkies had been beaten in Perth by Merv Adam's W A side and had drawn in Melbourne, so it was on the cards that they would be in for a tough game in Sydney.

From memory (I could be wrong), it was the very first

international game of hockey that was televised 'live' in Australia. It was at a dog track venue, 'Wentworth Park'. Not the best surface for the Pakkies, and because of the dog track not very good for the spectators (too far from the playing area).

That year, the hockey authorities were determined to cut out 'dangerous play' so balls lifted into goal from a penalty corner off a direct hit were being disallowed if over the 18 inch high mark. This 'rule' had only just been tried out and the Pakkies were quite upset when three of their 'goals' were disallowed for being hit 'too high'! Where they played on the Indian Sub-continent the interpretation of 'dangerous' was if it 'hit someone on the way in' it was dangerous, but if it went in 'clean' it was usually awarded as a goal! Their crowds of unruly supporters would make any umpire think twice before he disallowed a goal. He could be manhandled by a mob if their team lost over a decision like that! With this as the background, I was not in the least bit surprised when Major Atif, the Pakkie Captain, led his team off the field, as he felt they were being cheated by the Aussie umpires.

This was sensational. It had never, to my knowledge, ever happened before in an International hockey match. The crowd of spectators were nonplussed and stunned! After a great deal of pleading and persuasion the Pakkies came back on. They then proceeded to pass the ball around the top of the Ozzie circle, with about five players touching it before it was pushed into the 'boards'. They then all turned and looked at the umpire as if to say 'how about that one?' The goal was awarded and they looked a lot happier, but not for long!

Australian ace centre half (in my view, Australia's greatest centre half) Julian Pearce, split the Pakkies defence with a beautifully weighted pass which Eric Pearce, our centre forward, ran on to, collected, and was about to shoot for goal when he was brought down in the circle in a nasty tackle to prevent him scoring! Without any hesitation, the umpire in control awarded a penalty stroke. That was the signal for another show of petulance, and the Pakkies stormed off the field for the second time in a disgraceful manner.

Again it was a matter of 'interpretation'. They felt that, since their keeper was still in the net 'a certain goal' was not on, as this was their last line of defence, and he might have saved the shot. The rules, read differently in those days, and were thus open to different interpretations!

A good ten minutes elapsed and an 'International incident' could have developed when the players were finally persuaded back onto the field to finish the game, by the Pakistan High Commissioner.

A strange thing had happened however. While the Pakkies were off the field (in protest) the umpire allowed the Aussies to shoot the ball into an empty goal to level the score. This was wrong in hindsight but there was so much confusion and shouting and carrying on, that the umpire, instead of abandoning the game and awarding the game on a forfeit to Australia, allowed them to take the 'stroke' with no opponent in the Pakkie net! Quite absurd!

At work the next day, people at my office said to me 'Trevor what an exciting game hockey is! But, by the way, do they walk off whenever they don't like the umpire's decision?' It was a shame as this, to my knowledge, was the first televised game of hockey in Australia, and there is no knowing the damage it did to the image of the game.

Within six months of our arrival in Australia my family and I had bought a home in North Manly, so I decided to play for the local Manly Hockey Club in Second Division. An ex-Glebe stalwart about the same age as myself, one Jack Taylor, was also in the same team as myself, which was a great help. I lost over a stone-and-a-half in weight to do justice to my effort in this team.

Because the younger ones were considered the future of the club they were in the First team. Jack and I were quite happy to play in the second team and teach the younger ones how to play competition hockey. We went on to win the Grand Final of our division that year and I was lucky to be presented with the club Best and Fairest prize for our team.

I was elated, but went back to the Glebe Club the following season. I did so because of the lack of genuine interest in training exhibited by the Manly group. The Glebe boys were happy to have me back, and Nilan, Westacott, Needham and Gillie were responsible for getting me a place in their top team for the pre-season Bisley Shield tourney.

One day at training a young player called Don Barker from Perth, Western Australia, wandered over to the Glebe ground and asked for a game. He had been in the strong WA Senior squad so he knew how to play. He was doing his National Service and that was why he was in Sydney. We welcomed him into the club.

That year Glebe had ex-international Queenslander Dessie Wise playing centre-half, Don Barker left-half and myself playing right-half. We had veteran Kenny Wark as skipper and full-back. With Pat Nilan, Vic Westacott, Bennet Dunn, Russ Nicholls and Charlie Brown on the wing we won the Grand Final of the Bisley Shield. I still have the pennant to prove it.

When the season proper started Wise, Nicholls and I reverted to second grade and we won this grade two years in a row. We were an awesome backup to our First grade side, which was already feared by all the other teams in the Sydney competition! The drinking and fun we had in the clubrooms under the Arches was memorable. The feeling at the Club was one of love for the game of Hockey and genuine mateship. Our mutual ties were so strong that many years later, when I was Director of Coaching in Canberra for the ACT Hockey Association, the Glebe Club invited me to be a guest speaker at their Annual Dinner, an invitation I gladly accepted.

SOME GOLDEN GLEBE MEMORIES

Watching and listening to Graeme (Gillie) Gilmore coach the juniors at Glebe was a real delight. His rapport with the kids was amazing. They cottoned on so very quickly! This showed me why the Glebe Club was always full of star-quality players coming through the pipeline, and why the Club had maintained its strong position in Sydney for over fifty years. Gillie was a drummer in a rock band by night and was a rep for a photographic company by day. His wit and humour were always evident. He played a mean game of hockey at full back alongside Ken Wark, himself an all time great, and the influence of Nilan and Westacott came through in his game.

Quite early in my stay in Sydney during a beer after a game I happened to ask, 'How do you keep your lawns so well appointed?' The answer was so simple: 'Cut the grass!' I had never owned a lawnmower in my life, as we had not lived in a house with a lawn before. In India we had been living in flats. On my looking a bit puzzled, Bennet Dunn immediately offered to loan me his lawnmower, and teach me how to use it. I never forgot that kindness!

Another unforgettable memory was Ken Wark saying to me that he had always admired an Anglo-Indian player who had emigrated to Sydney in the early 50s: Dick Carr. Dick had won an Olympic Gold Medal while playing for India. In fact, Dick Carr was one of the best-ever players to come from India to Australia, and had played with the great Indian wizard Dhyan Chand himself!

HEROES OF GLEBE

THE WARK CLAN

I am proud to say that the skipper of my very first team in Australia, the Glebe Second Division team, was Harry Wark, one of the two famous Wark brothers, both Glebe players. His brother was Kenny Wark, the ex-international player, who was still in First grade. His son, Ken Wark Jnr. later played for Australia and was a star full-back.

Molly Wark was a Club stalwart and Life Member. She was an inspiration to her husband and brother-in-law as well as to her sons and nephews, all of whom played for the Club. She also starred in the first Glebe Women's Hockey team.

The two Wark brothers (Senior) were feared in their day as First grade players. They were no-nonsense, tough, skilful players who could dish it out as well as take it. If an opponent on the field got 'touched up' and needed medical attention after clashing with a Wark, the opposition supporters would yell out 'You bloody butcher, Wark!' The remark was easily overlooked, as in fact Harry ran a butcher's shop.

VICTOR WESTACOTT

One of the Glebe stalwarts whom I greatly admired was Vic Westacott. Vic ran a wholesale spectacle-frame business. When I met him he was past his best, but still a mighty good hockey player who wore specs like myself while playing. On hearing I was from India he told me he had been immensely impressed by an Indian player called Babu who had toured Australia with the Indian Wanderers a few years before. 'Babu', in fact, was the great K. D. Singh, who had skippered the Gold Medal Winning 1952 Indian Olympic hockey team. His dazzling stick-work and all-round skill was of the highest order. I had once seen him play in Calcutta in the Beighton Cup, and though he was by then quite out of condition, he was still a handful of skill and guile for his UP XI team.

I had to agree with Vic. 'Babu', as K. D. Singh was called, was an ornament to the game. How sad it was, and what a shock, to read some years later, that when India lost to Australia in the penalty flick shoot-out in the Montreal Olympic Semi-Final in 1976, 'Babu', who had been listening to the radio broadcast of the match, put a gun to his head and blew his brains out! He could not bear to hear that India had lost.

PAT NILAN

Glebe Seniors NSW/Australia

Pat was referred to as 'Mister Hockey' in the Sydney press due to his valuable contribution to hockey. He was formally rewarded with the Order of Australia (O.A.), and it was fully deserved. A wonderful player with silky skills reminiscent of the great Indian forwards of any era. Stick work, passing, shot on goal, working back in defence, tackling, etc. The complete player in the opinion of all the experts. Pat was to Australian hockey in the sixties what Ric Charlesworth was in the seventies. Nilan went to three Olympics.

GRAEME GILMORE

Glebe Senior Player/Junior Coach

When I first set eyes on Gillie he was playing left fullback to Kenny Wark Snr. in the Glebe first team. He looked skinny but was as tough as nails. A good tackler and reader of the play. Talked a lot, both on and off the field. Very encouraging to the younger members of the team. Great team man. 'An amazing example of devotion above and beyond the call of duty!' was the quote from the Glebe History book Under the Arches.

Gillie coached the Glebe Under 10's for seventeen consecutive seasons, so was an invaluable member of the Glebe Hockey Club. One of Graeme's reports mentioned that his U/10's side played 'In the fine traditions of the Club! Tradition, commitment, a sense of history, effort trying, and attitude!' These were all qualities that Graeme instilled in his charges over the long period that he coached his young teams. Remember they were only nine-year-olds! Is it any wonder that the Glebe Hockey Club produced such good hockey players over the years? Champions such as Pat Nilan, Ken Wark Snr., Ken Jnr., Vic Westacott, Charlie Brown, Lenny Needham, Billy Stubbs and Pat Dunne…the list is endless and includes Warren (Buster) Birmingham rated at one stage to be the best centre-half in the world!

In summary I am proud to say, as are all Glebe players, *'I played with Glebe!'*

My job with Gestetner in Sydney was going well. I had been promoted to selling machines as well as supplies. After two years of working hard at it the news was that the parent company in the UK was about to open an assembly plant in New Zealand.

I at once thought of the words of my then (1959) Tottenham factory Assistant Chemist (Cyril Green) under whom I trained in the UK. 'Trevor! If ever there is anything I can do for you in the future, please feel free to contact me!' Well, seven years on, he was now Chief Chemist. So I wrote to him asking him to consider my name for the position of Plant manager of the proposed set-up in Auckland.

I was qualified for the job, having done the same work as Works Manager in the Entally plant in Calcutta, from 1960 to 1964, that is, up to the time I emigrated to Australia for the betterment of my family's future. David Gestetner (grandson of the founder) came to Sydney and announced in the Aussie Country managers office that the London Board had appointed me as their new factory manager in New Zealand. Cyril Green had kept his word and had recommended my name for the job.

Well, the 'sh★★t hit the fan!' The Aussie GM was not impressed that I had approached London without his knowledge (a breach of protocol I suppose). He tried strenuously to oppose my appointment. David Gestetner sensed this and then firmly laid the law down. The London Board had made the appointment and that was that. 'Trevor, go home right now and give your wife Jean the good news. I'll see you in London when you come for a short refresher course in about six weeks. Both Cyril Green and your old Boss in India, Ronnie Watson, send you their regards and congratulations.' I was on cloud nine as I raced home to give Jean the good news!

All this happened on the 1st of September 1966. We were off to New Zealand for another start in a decent job with the firm I had loyally served since I had started out as a young 18 year old…or so I thought! Well! My hopes were dashed when on Christmas Eve that year, at the break-up office party, Gestetner London's telex arrived. The whole New Zealand venture was cancelled, it said, because the New Zealand government would not agree to the repatriation of profits overseas, due to the shortage of foreign exchange in New Zealand at the time. My dream was shattered! In addition, I was sure the General Manager, who had opposed my promotion anyway, would have it in for me. I decided I must move on and find another job after the Christmas break.

I saw an ad in the Sydney papers while still on holiday and applied for a position with Remington Rand as a Sales

Executive in their Rex Rotary Duplicator division. I got the job, but insisted that I be allowed to give proper notice to the firm that had helped me with a job when I was new in the country.

I started with Remingtons in the first week of April 1967. After having worked for Gestetner for over sixteen years, starting at a new company made me a little apprehensive on my first day at Remingtons. The cultures were different. One was a British company with solid traditions, while the other was an American company with its razzamatazz sales meetings and shortcuts to Get-the-sale-at-all-costs attitude. This at least suited me at the time.

I was initially told when interviewed for the position that I had to prove myself, and if I 'kept my nose clean' I would be considered for promotion in this large worldwide conglomerate. I did reasonably well, and Remington kept their word. After two years, I was promoted to the position of Sales Manager of the Reprographics Division (Duplicators and Offset) in West Australia.

David Bell, Australian Captain, receiving the World Cup, 1986.
Courtesy of *Hockey Australia*.

Top: Colin Batch and Terry Walsh after Terry scored the first goal in the World Cup 86 final.
Bottom: Coach Aggiss with World Cup 86.
All Pictures courtesy of *Hockey Australia*.

Top Left: Treva King embraces 'Charlie' after World Cup 86 final whistle.
Top Right: 'Charlie' shows his Best Player award.
Bottom: 'Charlie' Charlesworth pleads with ref.
All Pictures courtesy of *Hockey Australia*.

Top: 'Charlie shows his class'
Bottom: 'Charlie' shows what 'effort' is/
All Pictures courtesy of *Hockey Australia.*

Australia, 1986 World Cup Winners.

Back, Left to Right: Mark Hager, John Bestal, Neil Hawgood, Tony Galvin (Doctor), Graham Reid (Physiotherapist), Grant Mitton, Neil Snowden, Craig Davies, Colin Batch, Adrian Berce, Peter Haselhurst, Warren Birmingham.

Front, Left to Right: Ken Wark, Terry Walsh, Alan Berry (Team Manager), David Bell (Captain), Treva King (Vice-Captain), Richard Aggiss (Coach), Richard Charlesworth, Dean Evans.

Top Left: Grandmother Marie Milner, Aunty Violet and myself in "Green Ridges"
Top Right: My Dad's sister Aunt Marie, Chairwoman of the Ranchi Flower Show, showing Prime Minister Indira Gandhi around.
Bottom: Pony ride with Aunt Marie's Syce (horse-handler).

Top: Me, complete with umbrella.
Bottom: Kenchinjunga from the mall in Darjeeling.

Top: Race Course, Darjeeling. "Ghoom"
Bottom: "Toy Train" to Darjeeling.

Top: Marie Milner (my great-grandmother, daughter of Henry Caversham). Marie Milner (my grandmother, married to my grandfather Alec Vanderputt). Edward 'Ted' Vanderputt (my father, standing). Faye Vanderputt-Stevens (my sister). Lynn Stevens (my niece, Faye's daughter).
Bottom Left: My first school blazer.
Bottom Right: My first hockey trophy.

Top: Group of mates. Myself (2nd from right, standing), and my brother Neville (2nd from left, sitting).
Bottom: St Edward's High School 1st XI. Simla, India, circa 1947. (Author standing 4th from left)

Top: Yachts on Naini Tal Lake circa 1948.
Bottom: St Joseph's College Hockey 1st XI 1948
(Author: back row, second from right).

Top: St Joseph's College Classes 9 and 10 (Author: Back row, far right).
Bottom: 'P & O' Stratheden.

Pat Jansen, Rest in Peace!

Top Left: Dhyan Chand, 1967.
Top Right: The "Hockey Twins" Dhyan Chand and his brother Roop Singh.
Bottom: Lt. Col. John Fonseca and the Indian Armed
Services Hockey Team , 1965.

Left: Dhyan 'The Wizard' Chand.
Right: Dhyan Chand with Mrs G, C. Fletcher during an exhibition match in Calcutta 1949.

Top: (Left to Right) Paul, Dean, Barry and Floyd: My four sons in their St Joseph's Blazers circa 1964.
Bottom: Vanderputt Family circa 1959.

Gestetner Hockey Team, winners of the Calcutta Office League – Mussle White Cup. Claude Weil (center, front) was the grandson of company founder David Gestetner. Roy Tamplin (on Claude's left) was Works Manager – India. (Author: Roy's left).

Top: On board SS Stratheden.
Bottom Left: With Barney Kinder at Port Said, 1949.
Bottom Right: On Stratheden in Red Sea (Author: In the middle).

Left: India's 1936 Olympic Team. Dhyan on Keeper Allen's right, Joe Gallibardy sitting on the ground in front. *Right:* Leslie Claudius. Four times Indian Olympian (3 Gold, 1 Silver)

Bengal Captains
Top Left: A, L. Hosie, 1926
Top Right: F, C. Wells, 1928
Bottom Left: Shaukat Ali, 1932
Bottom Right: C. Tapsell, 1936 and 1944

Top: Australian Olympic Team 1968.
Bottom: Massive crowd at Mardeka Stadium, Kuala Lumur, for the World Cup Final, 1975, between India and Pakistan.

Top: Glebe's most famous family: The Warks.
Left to Right: Harry and Ken snr, Robert, Les, Gary and Ken jnr (15). Harry junior was overseas when this photo was taken.
Bottom: Pat Nilan.

Top Left: Ken Wark, Jnr.
Top Right: Author receiving the winning pennant from Glebe stalwart Jack Taylor.
Middle Right: Author receiving Manly-Warringa, Hockey Club's 'Best and Fairest' trophy in 1966.
Bottom: Under the Arches

Hockey
DOWNUNDER

Top: Hockey Down-under
Bottom: The Premiership winning side of 1964
Left to Right: Robert "Charlie" Brown, Ken Wark, Dennis Lisk, David "Davy Crockett" Crocker, Greg Harris, Len Needham, Pat Nilan, Bennett Dunn, David Lisk, Victor Westacott and Frank Vanderputt (Goalie.)

Delhi Independents 2nd team. Author standing 3rd from the left.

Top: Delhi Anglo-Indian team playing under the name of UK High Comm.
(Author: Front, extreme left)
Bottom: Calcutta Rangers 1-B side winners of the Langdon Shield. Farley Baker, sitting extreme left, Fred Gormanly (Capt.) next to Baker. Charles Crizzle, standing extreme left. Lional Blanche (Club President.)
Desmond Holder on Blanche's left.

Bengal Captains
Top Left: Keshav Datt, 1950
Top Right: p. Da Luz, 1951 and 1952
Bottom Left: T. Mendies, 1958
Bottom Right: L. Claudius, 1953-57 and 1959-60

Bengal Captains
Top Left: R, J. Allen, 1938 and 1940.
Top Right: R, J. Carr, 1945 and 1947.
Bottom Left: C. Hodges, 1946
Bottom Right: P. Jansen, 1948 and 1949

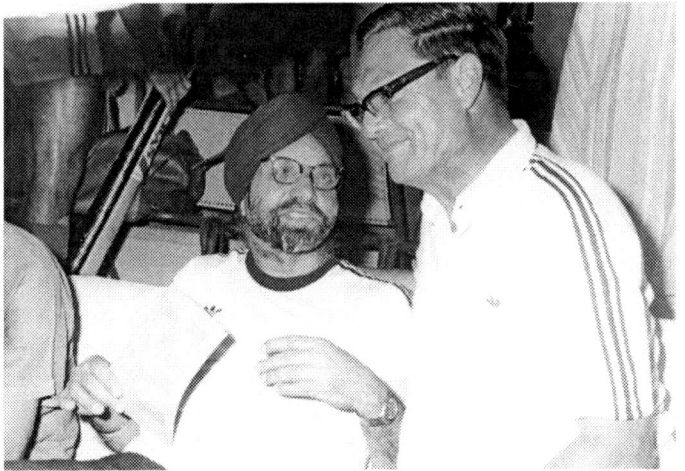

Author and hockey officials at Shivaji stadium, New Delhi, 1978.

Cricketers - 1978

FRONT ROW : Left to Right

DAVID LOCKETT, JOHN DAVIDSON, RIC CHARLESWORTH (Capt.—Coach), GLEN CARLSON, GEOF HASELHURST, RUSS HEARNDEN & ANDREW BARKER.

BACK ROW : Left to Right

ROBBIE McFARLANE, CRAIG DAVIES (Vice Capt.), CHRIS STACEY, GREG LANCASTER, JOHN CHARLICH & ALAN OSBORNE.

RIC CHARLESWORTH
(CAPT-COACH)

Cricketers' Hockey Club, 1978.

Left: Richard (Dick) Aggiss.
Top, Middle: Andrew Dean.
Bottom, Middle: "My Three Sons" with Don Corbitt (Extreme Right.)
Right: Frank Murray.

Top: Craig Davies in action.
Bottom: Terry Leese would go on to win the Champions Trophy in Pakistan. The team is seen here with President Zia ul Haq.

Peter Haselhurst.

Left: Treva King, left-half, beautifully balanced and reverse-side, collecting the ball with his trademark skill.
Right: Gordon Getley

Cricketers' at New Delhi, 1978.

Captain for the day: Bevan Lawrence (with headband, front, center). Other stars in the picture: Chris Stacey, Peter Haselhurst, Steve Hayward, Craig Boyce and Glen Carlson (Goalkeeper.) Other players to note: Geoff Hasselhurst, Rod Bell, Lancaster and Denis Reynolds. Richard Charlesworth was rested for this game.

Perth, Cricketer's Hockey Club, Lower grade teams in the 1980's.
Top: A-2'n Second Top Side. (Ex-Calcutta Rangers Club player Bill Leavers standing 2nd from right, back row. Rob McFarlane (front, left), 'Dinga' Gordon Bell (front, second from left), and Greg Black (extreme right).
Bottom: Australian Test Fast Bowler, Graham McKenzie (extreme right, standing), John Davidson (standing, extreme left). Author " helping out" with goalies pads (extreme left, kneeling).

The proud Cricketers' Hockey Club of WA in the 1970's.
Top: Bunbury Carnival.
Bottom: Goldy's (Dark Top) Vets.

Top Left: Richard Charlesworth.
Top Right: Richard Charlesworth, wife Frances and family: early 80's.
Bottom: Cricketers' Hocky Club, 1970's, Under 16's. (Peter Hasselhurst sitting 2nd from left)

Left: John Bestall.
Right: Damien Hicks.

Left: Mike Nobbs.
Right: Michelle with husband Mark Hager, the ace center-forward.

LIFE AFTER HOCKEY: Craig Davies will be able to devote more time to his wife Jenny and sons Christopher, 9, and Jason, 6. Picture: MOGENS JOHANSEN

Craig Davies with family.

Top Left: Richard Charlesworth swerving past a Pakistan player. (David Bell in Background.)
Top Right: Colin Batch in full flight.
Bottom Left: Michael Nobbs, One of the great players of the era 1980 to 1995.
Bottom Right: Terry Walsh (facing , with heavily strapped knee) after scoring a goal in the World Cup Final. John Bestall (No.5) races to congratulate him.

University A1 Grade Hockey Team Showing Syd Johnson (Capt. With cup) and Dennis Dunbar (Coach)

Top: WA State team 1948 off to Queensland. Some of the stars are shown: Ivan Mead, Gren Davies, Brian Strack, Dave Dick.
Bottom: West Australian Hockey Team.

MERV ADAMS

A gifted man who was able to impart his knowledge and experience to others with great skill.

Merv Adams, WA's most successful coach.

Top: The Aquinians A Grade hockey team of the 1930's relied almost entirely upon members of one family for its defence – the four Kennedy brothers.
Bottom: Peter, Neil, Dick and Ken Kennedy, seen talking together.

Top: 1930's University Hocky Team.
Bottom: Cricketers Hocky Club 1931.

Australian Senior Team at the Esanda Perth Hocky Tournament, 1979

Left: WA State U/16 Championship team. Author: extreme left, standing. Manager Howard Bradfield: standing extreme right. *Right*: Steve (Doc) Hayward. Inaugural WA Olympians Medal winner.

Top: Victorian U-14 Hockey Team. Australian Championships, Hobart, 1981.
Team (Starting Top Left): D Van Velzen, L Dreher, P. Donato, D. Horvath,
D. Symss, G. Jansz, P. Geddes, E. Eddings, T. Vanderputt (Coach), R. Clarke
(Captain), s. Purcell (V. Captain), K. Wensor (Manager), D. Blair, S. Siesmaa, P.
Marshman, R. Jones, S. Dempsey, J. Stacey.
Middle: Victorian Premiers. Camberwell, 1932.
Bottom Left: David Warnsbrough outstrips an Indian player, While
Colin Batch looks on
Bottom Right: Kim Harrison (facing camera) was one of a number of outstanding
Victorian administrators of the 1980's.

Graham Reid in action.

Superb Australian Goalkeeper Graham Reid, a Canberra product. His Club
(United H/C) kept playing him in the half-line.

Left: "Perhaps Trevor's major achievment was the establishment of *Minkey* in Canberra. *Minkey* started in 1982 with 12 teams and finished with 130 teams in 1984…"
Right: Graeme Reid, Australian Keeper.

Top: The Indian Wanderers in Camberwell, star Bhola striking the ball.
Middle: Victorian Under-Age Indoor Tournament winners, 1980.
Lachlan Dreher triumphantly wears the pads, while Jay Stacey stands on the extreme right.
Bottom: Dreher and Stacey get ready to leave for the Atlanta Olympics.

Top: Charlie Morley (seated on the ground, extreme left) and the Camberwell team of the 1940's.
Bottom: Don Argus, Senior Coach of the Camberwell Hockey Club in the 1980's.

Top: Mark Hagar and Ori Gasparini both playing in the forward ine for Australia U/21's.
Bottom: Steve Purcell playing left wing for the Victorian state team.

Left: Keith Murton (Olympic Team Manager, 1976).
Right: Steve Purcell playing left wing for the Australian U/21's.

Top: WA Junior Hockey Team, 1973.
This team includes C. Davies, P. Haselhurst and T. Leece, who went on to play in the Olympics for Australia.
Bottom: Western Australia Colts, 1976. Australian Hockey Championships.
Davies, Haselhurst, Leece, Boyce and Hayward all went on to represent Australia as senior internationals.

Top: Manager Howard Bradford and author after the triumphant U/16 Championship series.
Bottom: ACT State U/17's, including Abrahams, Carter, Aldrons, Andrew Dean and David Vanderputt, the author's son.

Top: Canberra U/14 Girls' Schools Team 1984. Katrina Powell is standing second from left in the front row. In this picture she is twelve years old.
Bottom: The famous picture above, of course, shows Katrina in the Olympic gold-medal-winning Australian team

CHAPTER FIVE: WESTERN AUSTRALIA

After five years in Sydney the move to Perth was quite dramatic for my young family. Jean had recently given birth to our fifth son, David. I went on ahead, the rest of the family staying behind till the kids had finished their school term. In hindsight it seems a completely unfair impost to inflict upon my wife, left on her own to complete the sale of the house, the packing and all the other work involved in the massive move to a new city on the other side of the continent. To her immense credit, she more than coped, and eventually caught the train with the five kids for the trip across the Nullarbor. I met my family at the Perth rail terminal and took them to the old house in South Perth that I had rented. Its main advantage was that it was a mere fifteen minutes' drive to work in the city in peak hour! All this took place in 1969.

Perth is a beautiful city built mainly on the Swan River, up-river from Fremantle on the Indian Ocean. My boys and I joined the Cricketers' Hockey Club, which had originated as a fitness club for off-season Cricketers. With my background of hockey, both in India and in the Glebe Hockey Club, we were made very welcome by the then President Mal Andrew and the Secretary Jim Black. Mal's son Bob was the Club Captain of the Senior team and was a fine, upstanding, disciplined hockey player who had already represented Australia at National level. He later went on to be a 1972 Olympian and went to Munich for the Games.

The Club ground was at College Park in the suburb of

Nedlands, one of the nicer Perth suburbs. Nevertheless I was in for a surprise. When I turned up for training one Tuesday evening straight from work I asked a fellow player, 'Where does one change?'

'Behind that tree,' was the reply, and of course I thought this was a smart-mouthed kid. 'Where are the toilets?' I repeated. 'Behind that other tree,' he grinned.

I was really browned off. Here was a so-called top-rated club in Perth without proper change-rooms or toilet facilities and this was 1969! Not a good start. The truth was that the local Council did provide a change-room and toilets but I cannot remember them ever being open for training nights.

Years later the club moved to Malvista, which was a much better facility. It had a beautiful view over the Swan River with good change-room and kitchen facilities.

In 1971 I was made captain of the B1s (I was now 40!) and we had a most enjoyable season, ending as runners-up in the Grand Final of the Pennant season. Meanwhile our top side was doing very well, and included players of the calibre of Ross Edwards (also a future cricket Test player), Laurie (the Mongrel) Bedford, Dick (Speedy) Osbourne, Peter Peterson and a young medical student named Richard Charlesworth. When I joined the Club, 'Charlie', as Charlesworth was affectionately called, was brilliant for his age and experience but was always very reluctant to pass the ball.

At the half-time talk at a certain 1A game, after Bob Andrew the skipper had had his say, he asked the Mongrel (Laurie Bedford) to say a few words.

He said: 'In this half, Charlie, if you don't pass the ball, I will drill it up your a**e first chance I get!'

Charlie was still a Colt (under 21) with John Goldie as his coach. Goldie had predicted to me and to all and sundry that Charlesworth would one day play for Australia. I of course went one better. I told Lester Charlesworth the dentist (Charlie's father) that his son would not only play for Australia but would one day Captain his country's hockey team. Both our predictions came to pass sooner than we thought possible.

Because I showed a lot of interest in our junior players, (remember I had four sons playing), Jim Black put my name forward to the Hockey Association to be considered for the position of State Under/16 Coach.

I was appointed to coach the U/16's in 1973. West Australia regularly won most Senior Inter-State Championships but somehow did not do very well in the Junior and Colts championships so this was a challenge to me to produce a winning team for a change.

That year (1973) my Juniors got to Canberra for the championships and we won undefeated. The skipper was Craig Davies who went on to play for Australia and also to Captain the National team some years later. Two others in that side went on to play for Australia: Peter Haselhurst and Terry Leese.

We finished second in the Championships in 1974 and 1975 as well. So the following year, when John Goldie gave up the Colts job due to work commitments, I was appointed as the Colts Coach. Not only did I have Davies, Haselhurst and Leese on my team again, but I also had Grant Boyce and Steve Hayward (the Captain) in the side as well. We did not win the Colts Championships in 1976, losing in extra time to Queensland in the Semi-Final, but all five players went on to play for Australia with distinction.

KUALA LUMPUR

The World Cup was to be played in K.L. in 1975. Australia had rebuilt the team that had missed a top-four placing by being beaten twice before the Semi-Finals in Munich. Younger players like David Bell, Terry Walsh, Mal Poole and Barry Dancer were the new hopes for Australia. Ric Charlesworth had now had three years' experience at this highest level, while Greg Browning was still young and raring to go. With Charlie there at right-inside Browning was forced to play on the right wing. Merv Adams was the new coach and expectations were really high that the team would do well.

I decided to go to K.L., and was accompanied by a young Perth lawyer named Bevan Lawrence, a keen hockey player and supporter. I took my son Barry who was fifteen and his hockey mate, Andrew Barker, on the trip so they would have each other's company and also experience both good hockey and also a foreign culture. The incessant rain almost completely disrupted the tournament. However, the games went on, but at the end of the round-robin series Australia missed out on the Semi-Finals. India went on to beat Pakistan in the final with a disputed goal.

The Australians were very disappointing. Both centre-forwards tried by coach Adams, Walter and Golder, were not at their best. Browning kept complaining that Charlie would not pass him the ball, but the loss wasn't Charlie's fault. Charlesworth was adequate in his role, and Sundance (Greg Browning) showed he was the best forward in the team when he got the ball. Herbie Haigh played brilliantly at left half-back, but it was only when he finally went to centre-half and Dancer was brought in as left-half that the team started to look good. However, the change was made too late. We had lost too many points early and so missed out on the Medal games (the Semi-Finals).

When the team returned to Perth, Adams stepped off the plane to state that we would win the Gold Medal at the following year's Olympics. He was re-appointed as coach but it was not to be! Australia lost to New Zealand in the Gold Medal match and thus won a Silver Medal at the Montreal Games. Adams was heartbroken when not re-appointed as coach. He applied for the National Women's Team coaching position and got the job.

It was like a new life to Merv! Up to this point in the long history of Australian Hockey for Women, the National team had never qualified for any International tournament. Merv Adams took them this important step forward. In a qualifying tournament in Vancouver, Canada, the team under Adams duly made it.

Merv suffered a heart attack the day after the tournament and died a few days later. At the memorial service held in Perth sometime later the Perth hockey fraternity turned out in their numbers to honour this great servant of Australian Hockey. Adams, with his infectious smile and easygoing manner, had made a lot of friends and a lot of ordinary hockey players into champions. It was fitting to see one of his protégés, Richard Aggiss, take over from him, first at State level (WA), then into the top coaching position in Australia.

Due to pressure from our Federal Government Australia did not participate at the Moscow Olympics. This was a great shame, as we had a good team with a new coach and had every chance of winning the gold medal.

CRICKETERS' TO INDIA, 1978

On being appointed Club Captain I felt this was the year Cricketers' should do things other Perth hockey clubs had so far been unable to do. My friend Merv Adams, the just-deposed National Coach, was also keen to do something out of the ordinary to revive his hockey standing in West Australia. We used to imbibe a few beers together at the Highway Hotel, and together we hatched plans to take a team on a tour that would give our senior players and soon-to-be senior players the opportunity and experience of playing in the country that had up until then the best hockey credentials of all: India!

With my contacts on the sub-continent I was the natural choice as the organizer of this venture. The plan was to take players drawn mainly from the Cricketers' Club and fill in positions for the players who were unable to make the trip with players from other clubs.

The team was very carefully chosen by Merv and myself. Craig Davies and Bob Andrew, two of our best, were unavailable, so we approached Steve Hayward (Fremantle Hockey Club) and Craig Boyce (YMCA). Both jumped at the invitation. We also picked up Bevan Lawrence (Freo), Denis Reynolds (Uni), Geoff Robinson (Modernians), and Rod Bell (Aquinas). Ric Charlesworth was to be Captain/Coach, and his eager acceptance and enthusiasm did a lot to make the tour one that players were keen to be a part of. John Goldie and Merv Adams were late withdrawals, so it was up to me to see that everything went off well and as planned.

The Club had previously restricted its 'trips' to short-haul journeys like Bunbury and Northam. I arranged a rather longer trip to Kalgoorlie in preparation for the next trip, which was to be a much bigger affair. We went up on the Prospector train and had a wonderful time.

For the journey to India passports, uniforms, fund-raising events and letters to my contacts in India had to be organised. Flights had to be co-ordinated with matches. Formal permission from our local Association and also the Australian Hockey Association had to be obtained. All this went off without a major hitch, and finally we were on our way!

Some Tour Memories

Madras: Very hot when we got off the plane! Game against a Madras Selected Eleven was fast and Charlie and Peter Haselhurst were in fine form. We won 2-1. I made a presentation to their best player, an Anglo-Indian centre-half. Our Hotel, the Connemara, was very comfortable and the food was very good and varied.

Calcutta: We got to Calcutta the same day that the monsoon broke. The trip in a very old bus from Dum Dum airport through the heart of old Calcutta to our hotel, the Grand, was through rain-filled streets flooded as the drains could not cope. The lads in the bus were singing in unison 'Welcome Home, Bunny' as they knew I was born in Calcutta. (My nickname was Bunny).

Game One was against the champions Mohun Bagan captained by my old opponent from the fifties Gurbux Singh (now 40 years old and still a fine player.) He had captained India at the Mexico Olympics and was one of the best fullbacks in the world. Charlie and the boys were superb and helped to win a tough game against Bengal's best.

Next day we were rostered to play the East Bengal Hockey Club, the Number Two team in Calcutta. Two penalty strokes were awarded against us early in the game so we had to play from 0-2 down. Charlie was at his best, even though he played with a heavily strapped thigh. The boys pulled one goal back but we were well held and the match ended with us losing 1-2 in a close game. The opposing coach, another old contemporary of my playing days, Surinder Singh was elated, but came up to me and apologised at the poor and biased umpiring. He handed us a magnificent trophy to remind us of the game. At the end of the game the heavens opened and the blinding rain almost made us miss our flight to New Delhi.

In this hurried departure from Calcutta David Charlesworth, our Assistant Manager, managed to lose his passport! On the bus to Dum Dum airport Charlie was kept very busy dispensing pills to those who had over-indulged in 'Tootie-Fruities', the delicious ice-cream served in the Grand Hotel in Calcutta. We caught an Airbus to New

Delhi.

New Delhi: The Ashok Hotel. A magnificent palace-like structure where the accommodation was really comfortable and the food was fantastic. The lads loved the tennis courts, swimming pool and endless supply of cold soft drinks that a sponsor had supplied, free of cost, to the team! Meanwhile the Grand Hotel in Calcutta had found David Charlesworth's passport and had it delivered to us in Delhi.

We had a few free days in Delhi so we went to Agra, city of the world famous Taj Mahal. We set off on the four-hour train journey, another Indian experience to remember for the lads. The Ashok Hotel people provided each player with a picnic lunch. We got back to Delhi around midnight pretty tired. There had been a mix-up in the travel arrangements, and consequently there was no waiting bus to take us to the hotel, but we soon boarded taxis and got back to our rooms worn out after a long day.

A few of the guys decided to hire a car and go to a town in the Punjab called Jullunder where the hockey sticks were made. Luckily for them the hired car came with a driver, otherwise the trip on the Grand Trunk Road may have proved disastrous, the truck traffic and potholes were so dangerous! A game was arranged at a town called Meerut about two hours drive from Delhi. This allowed us to give the extra players in the squad a game.

They also got a game in the Delhi match which was hurriedly arranged. Charlie did not play in these two games to give his thigh a chance to recover from the strain he had picked up in Calcutta. Bevan Lawrence captained the side and wore a head bandana, which led the locals to believe he was in fact Charlie! (Charlie always played with a bandana.) Rod Bell scored a fine goal and we ended up winning 2-0.

Bombay: the last stop on a very tiresome tour. The Australian Embassy staff in Delhi were very helpful when Ric Charlesworth lost his passport! Unbelievable that two guys on the tour should lose their passports and they were both named Charlesworth!

The *Taj Mahal* in Bombay was a five-star hotel overlooking the Gateway of India and the Arabian Sea.

The match against a selected eleven was always going to be tough, as it was to be played prior to the Final of the prestigious Bombay Invitation Tournament against a team selected from the teams that did not make the final. Our lads were really tired after a busy tour, and if it had not been for our goalkeeper Glen Carlson, and some tricky umpiring by our own umpire, we would have been beaten. As it turned out we drew the match and left next day for Perth, WA. All felt it was a worthwhile once-in-a-lifetime experience.

CRICKETERS' HOCKEY CLUB

Having four sons playing for the Club I was involved with the transporting of them to the various venues to play on Saturday mornings. On being invited to coach these juniors I opted to do the U/10's in which my youngest was playing.

These young ankle-biters were so keen it was a real pleasure teaching them the game. With their Mums on the sidelines cheering them on we were very successful in a very short time. I arranged a trip to play a school team in Geraldton, a town about 300 miles north of Perth. We went up for a weekend, playing a match on the Saturday and a return match on the Sunday. The opposition kids were at least a year or two older than our boys. Their physical strength took its toll and they won easily 5-0. That night we planned what we would do the next day and playing a 'system' which these country lads and their coach had never encountered before we beat them on the Sunday, much to the delight of our boys and their parents and the dismay of our opponents: players, coach and parents.

Those were great days on the banks of the Swan River at

Malvista Oval. After the Saturday matches, all Cricketers' teams returned to the club rooms to talk about the games and various other subjects. We used to sell 100 pies, 50 pasties and goodness knows how many soft drinks and cups of steaming hot coffee and tea. The club fielded five senior teams and four junior teams. All First team players, except for the State and international players, had to help coach selected juniors on a roster basis. Older players who had moved down the grades were a source of on-field coaching during match days, and this helped boost the depth of players in the club and prepare a steady stream of younger guys, all versed in the Cricketers' way of playing. This system kept Cricketers' Hockey Club at either the top or very near the top of WA hockey right through the 1970's, and produced Australian Senior Internationals of the calibre of Gordon Bell, Laurie Bedford, Robert Andrew, Ric Charlesworth, Graeme Walter, Peter Haselhurst and Craig Davies.

In the seventies in Perth, Western Australia, the top sides were: Cricketers', YMCA, University and Modernians. Later when Dick Aggiss left the Mods to try his hand at coaching, Old Aquinians became a power. Perth had a poultice of Internationals running around the various grounds. Names that spring to mind include Ray Evans, Julian and Gordon Pearce, Laurie Bedford, Gordon Bell, Bob Andrew, Graeme Walter, Mal Poole, Ron Wilson, Bryan Rourke, Brian Glencross, Mike O'Reilly, Dick Aggiss, David Bell, Steve Smith, Terry Walsh, Steve Hayward, Peter Haselhurst, Terry Leese, Craig Davies, Bruce Shannahan, Grant Boyce, John Bestall, Dean Evans, Don Smart, Don Martin and the incomparable Richard Charlesworth.

RICHARD CHARLESWORTH

Known as 'Ric' or 'Charlie'! Short and of stocky build. Very muscular and a fanatic for fitness! A student of the game and had showed potential very early. At age 16 played inside-right for Cricketers' Hockey Club in 1A's (top division in Perth.) Had huge shoes to fill in this position as Australian (Melbourne Olympics) hockey captain, the brilliant Ian Dick had played in this position for Cricketers' Hockey Club till an eye injury ended his playing days. Charlie played alongside internationals Robert (Bob) Andrew, Gordon (Dinga) Bell and Laurie (The Mongrel) Bedford. Ian Dick was a great passer of the ball and Charlie in 1969 was just the opposite! He wanted to 'beat' or 'dribble' everyone! I remember listening to the half-time talks! Laurie would be dragging away on a cigarette and Bob Andrew would be encouraging his players. When he had finished, like all good captain/coaches he'd turn to Laurie for his comments as I mentioned earlier.

Charlie was a medical student in University in 1969. Always broke! But loved coming to the pub (Highway in Nedlands) after training at College Park to listen to the hockey gossip and join in the fun. Only drank middies of squash and someone else (usually John Goldie) paid!

He felt he had a lot to live up to, as his father, Lester Charlesworth, had represented Western Australia in Cricket and was a successful dentist. Charlie went further! He represented Western Australia in cricket like his father before him (captained the Sheffield Shield side), became a Doctor (MD) and then went on to politics and was elected Federal Member of Parliament for Perth. His greatest love, however, was hockey. Played for and captained Australia in a long and distinguished hockey career which spanned five Olympic Games. Won a Silver Medal in Montreal (1976) and a Gold in the World Cup in London (1986).

A lot has been written already about Ric Charlesworth the state and international hockey player. I wish to write about Ric the club player, man, husband, father, son, brother and friend.

CLUB MAN

Charlie took over as Cricketers' Club Hockey 1A captain from the legendary 'Bob' Andrew. Bob had moved from left-inner (where he played in his early club and state hockey) to centre-half (Club) and right-half (State and Australia). Charlie led by example, and as a player and at training he never tolerated anything but the best effort a guy could give. 'If you want to play with this team (Cricketers') you will have to improve your performance or your position is in jeopardy!' This word 'jeopardy' was the catch-word in those years! Around training at Malvista Oval, under Charlie's guidance, players like Graeme (Ces) Walter, Peter Haselhurst and Craig Davies became successful Australian internationals, and players like Alan Osbourne, Chris Stacey, Kim Harrison, Glen Carlson, and Geoff Haselhurst, Dick (Speedy) Osborne, John Davidson, and John Hannaford made the State team for Western Australia.

John Goldie coached Charlie as a Colt, and Merv Adams coached him as a State and Australian player. Later McCormick and Richard Aggiss were his coaches over the many years he represented Australia. Bob Andrew, Jim Black and Ray Strauss were his earlier coaches and mentors.

I remember one incident in those early years at Cricketers' regarding a young goalkeeper, Glen Carlson, who hailed from a town called Bunbury about 200 km south of Perth in Western Australia. Glen had played state junior (U/16) in 1974 and I was his coach (WA junior) at the time. Because I saw great potential in Glen I persuaded his parents to let Glen travel to Perth to play hockey for

Cricketers' Club, Perth's top club at the time. This seemed a stiff task to play 2A's (second team).

Richard 'Speedy' Osbourne was the best keeper in the State. Some ranked him after Peter Shepherd, but in my opinion Speedy was better than 'Shep' on his good days! By 1975 Speedy 'discovered' and was courting his present wife Rosemary and what with teaching commitments decided to take a break from 1A hockey in 1976. In went young Glen ('Pimple-Face') Carlson.

While adjusting to top grade hockey (going from 2A's to 1A's), Glen had a few 'poor days' in the net and the usual murmurs were on! *Glen should be dropped!* Charlie heard this 'whisper' around the club and turned up to the 'selection meeting' at the Highway Hotel! He was very firm, and convinced all present that 'anyone who can travel 400 km a week every Tuesday for training and again on weekends for the Games and shows the kind of improvement and attitude that Glen Carlson shows - is in my team!' There was never another word said about Glen Carlson's ability to play 1A's for Cricketers'. Glen went on to play twenty seasons in 1A's! To my knowledge only Charlie himself (twenty seasons) has equalled the record and 'Doc' Hayward has come close with eighteen. 'Dinga' Bell played longer but not at 1A's.

FAMILY MAN

Charlie married Frances, the sister of 'Speedy' and Alan Osbourne, who also represented WA in women's hockey. Frances, with her country charm and love of both hockey and Ric, reared two lovely girls and a boy. With Ric busy playing either Sheffield Shield cricket or International hockey, and then later being Federal Member for Perth in Parliament with long stints in Canberra, all these commitments took their toll. Sadly, to those that knew both of them, the marriage broke up in 1985. Frances re-married and is still good friends with Richard, who sees his kids regularly and coaches their girls' hockey team.

As a son Charlie had a promise to keep to his father, a promise he wanted to keep more than anything else! This was to play for the University of WA's 1A team and to win a premiership or at least take University to a Grand Final. He achieved nearly all his goals. With players like 'Doc' Hayward, John Netteton, Denis Reynolds (now a Magistrate in WA), Lindsay Edmonds and WA Hockey Association President, Bob Brindley, Charlie took Uni to a Grand Final, like Frank Murray before him! But ironically on both occasions Uni went down to Ric's old Club, Cricketers'.

Charlie then had a season with 'rent-a-team' Suburban Hockey Club: 'subs' who had only recently made a comeback to 1A's. A club with a tradition 'as long as your arm', Suburban was a founder member of the WA Hockey Association. A rich club with a lot of professional men as members (doctors, lawyers, judges, teachers etc.)

The club had recruited wisely – Peter Freitag and Bob Cattrall, both ex-English Internationals, Mike Nobbs, Grant Mitton and David Francis from South Australia, Alan Kercher (ACT) and Steve College from Queensland – six international players and a good coach!

They won three premierships on the trot, and the hockey fraternity sat up and took notice of Peter Freitag as a coach who 'delivers the goods!' Peter went on to be appointed Assistant Coach of the Australian Women's Hockey Team and helped win the Gold Medal in Seoul.

Charlie then returned to his old club, Cricketers'. With Davies, Haselhurst and a squad of talented young 'turks' he won the premiership again before retiring in 1988. Charlie's last game was the Grand Final. He played centre-half and was judged 'best on the ground', winning the Adams Medal at the ripe old age of 37 years!

During his University days, at a time when he was considered an 'automatic choice' for the National Team, Charlie asked me, as Cricketers' Club Secretary, to write a letter on his behalf and present it to Eric Eastman, who was both President of the WA Hockey Association at the time and also an Australian Senior Selector. The letter informed the National Selection Committee that, due to Charlie's having his final exams to be a medico, he would not be available for the Tasmanian International match due to be played, but would be available for the New Zealand tour to take place straight after.

When the team for New Zealand was announced in the press, Charlie's name was not in it. Instead the press announcement had the comment 'unavailable due to medical exams.' Charlie was livid!

He requested the Club Committee to write a letter of protest as to why he should miss selection, when in fact his club had written Eastman a letter saying he was available for the New Zealand part of the event. I was Honorary Secretary of Cricketers' Hockey Club at the time so my signature was on the letter to the National Selectors' Committee, addressed to Eastman. I 'copped it' from Eastie! I was also the State Junior coach at the time. Eastman rang me up and promised me I'd never get another official hockey job in WA again! Because I had taken up the fight for Charlie, I was a marked man.

It turned out, as Eastman later told me, he had had the letter in his pocket at the selection meeting in Melbourne and had not even read it! Hence Charlie's omission!

CHAMPION

A legend! The greatest hockey player Australia ever produced and arguably one of the best the world has seen.

The Indians had Dhyan Chand, Penniger and Claudius; Australia had Richard Charlesworth.

Like Ron Clarke, the great Australian athlete who never won an Olympic Gold Medal, Charlie never won Olympic gold either as a player. However, he carried the Australian flag at the Seoul Olympics, an honour bestowed by the Australian Olympic Committee deservedly on this great hockey player of the era.

Many people accused Charlie of being arrogant and aloof sometimes. I always defended him against this wrong perception. Sure, Charlie did not suffer fools gladly and had little time for small talk, gossip and rumours. But I am proud to have been associated with Richard Charlesworth, both as a fellow club member and a friend. Charlie was a good friend to me.

In the late seventies and early eighties, when it appeared that if one wanted to play for Australia at Senior level one had to transfer and live in Perth to be noticed, we started getting players from other States who were hoping to make the Australian side. Some of the better ones to transfer to Perth were Barry Dancer and Steve Colledge from Queensland, and David Francis and Mike Nobbs from South Australia.

When the Australian Institute of Sport opened its Hockey Unit in Perth these names joined others like Warren Birmingham, Ken Wark and Steve Davies from New South Wales; Andrew Dean (Canberra); Grant Mitton (SA); Neil Hawgood (Queensland); Todd Williams (Tasmania) and Adrian Berse (SA). These players, under first Dick Aggiss and then more recently under Frank Murray, took Australian hockey to the top of the hockey world with the only trophy not on the shelf: the Olympic Gold Medal!

In summary: Not only did WA produce great hockey players, it also produced great Australian Captains such as

Donald Tregonning (1932), G. F. Milner (1937), Ian Dick (1956), Kevin Carton (1960), Brian Glencross (1972), Ric Charlesworth(1984), David Bell (1986) and Craig Davies (1988).

WA MEMORIES AND SNIPPETS

Barry Shepherd, the West Australian cricket captain, was a member of the famous Cricketers' Hockey Club and a prominent State hockey player as well, as was fellow member, Test and State cricketer, Ross Edwards.

Ross played in a WA State side under Merv Adams against the Pakistan hockey team when the Pakistanis visited Western Australia on their way to Tokyo for the 1964 Olympics. WA won that match and showed that Australia could beat the best in the world! Ross at left half was unbeatable, a fact that contributed greatly to the win.

Some of the best matches witnessed in Perth were some of the State Grand Finals of the 1970's, such as the ones between the Cricketers' and YMCA, Old Aquinians vs YMCA and the Cricketers' vs University.

The Cricketers' took the field against YMCA at Fletcher Park. This match occurred before the Hockey Stadium was built. Stars on that day were Terry Walsh, Brian Glencross, Grant and Craig Boyce for the Y, Ric Charlesworth, Bob (The Colonel) Andrew and Glen Carlson for Cricketers'. YMCA ran out winners after a mighty game.

The next really memorable Grand Final game was the Old Aquinians vs YMCA, at Stevens Reserve in Fremantle. This was a marathon game of splendid hockey, with two lots of extra time played to get a result. Several players from both sides went down with cramp as a consequence of outstanding effort. A wonderful and unforgettable Final! Aquinas won that game under Player-Coach Dick Aggiss. Stars for YMCA on the day were Terry Walsh and Craig Boyce, and for Aquinas Tex Prindiville, Richard Aggiss,

Richard McWilliam and WA Olympian David Bell.

The most spectacular Final I ever witnessed in WA was Cricketers' vs University played at McGillivray Oval on natural grass. University took the early lead under new coach, Frank Murray, with WA Olympian medal-winner, Steve (Doc) Hayward, hitting three penalty corners in the first half. Cricketers' got one back, but were down 1-3 at half time. I then heard one of the most inspiring half-time coaching talks ever from Richard Charlesworth who went out after the break and scored the finest hat-trick I was ever privileged to witness. Bob Andrew at centre-half and young Peter Haselhurst at inside-left were on fire, and with the inspiration from Charlie they won a memorable game. Final score 4-3 to Cricketers'.

The team I coached in 1976, the WA Colts (U/21s) was one of the strongest Colts sides ever to leave Perth for the National Colts Championships in Adelaide. The team from the back: John Nettleton in goal, Steve Hayward and Craig Davies full-backs, Rob McFarlane, Grant Boyce and Chris Stacey half-backs. Forwards were Peter Haselhurst, Terry Leese, Greg Davies, Peter Westerberg and Mike Pearce (son of the famous Eric Pearce.) Five members of this team went on to play for Australia. That's the calibre of players they were!

Astoundingly we did not win the title that year. We were beaten by Queensland in a sudden-death overtime in the semi-final by a goal scored after an uncharacteristic defensive lapse on the part of WA. The star of that game was Queensland future international, Treva King.

Being the coach, I really copped it on our return to Perth. I had to answer truthfully.

'How could you lose with a strong team like that?'
'We were not good enough on the day.'
'Who did they have in their team?'
'A guy called Treva King.'

'Never heard of him!'

'You will, I promise you!'

Treva King went on to represent Australia for many years and won a Gold Medal at the World Cup in 1986.

WAHA: THE POWER WIELDERS

In the mid-seventies, under President Colin Nicholas, a sub-committee was formed to look into all aspects of coaching. This high-powered group included Australian Coach Merv Adams, the Australian Captain Brian Glencross, Graeme Worth and Basil Warner, who had recently been appointed Development Officer. Also on the committee were the then Senior Coach of the WA Hockey Association (WAHA), Dick Aggiss, the Colts Coach John Goldie, and myself, Junior Coach Trevor Vanderputt.

In 1977 this group organized the first real live-in Coaching Seminar ever held in West Australia for clubs who were interested in improving their members' knowledge of hockey coaching. The response was really gratifying.

The Hockey Coaching Weekend Camp was held by the Ministry of Sports, Health and Recreation at Guildford. All senior coaches were rostered as instructors and the whole programme was coordinated by Basil Warner. In the opinion of many hockey enthusiasts this course was the first really conscious effort to coach the coaches!

The formation of the Coaching Committee, the Coaching Camp, and the consequent boom in hockey, especially in WA, was due in large measure to the string of highly dedicated and able administrators that brought West Australian hockey to the top of the hockey tree in Australia. Gordon Getley (pictured) was one of the more forceful WAHA presidents of the 1980s.

The Presidents of the Hockey Association of Western Australia in the seventies were Dick Faulds, Eric Eastman and Colin Nicholas. Another fine administrator was Bruce Goodheart, the leading light of a group called the Hotspurs, known affectionately as the Godfather to his mates and fellow-Hotspurs. Mike Kinsella, Rodney Rate, Charles Harper and Vern Gooch were all active and wonderful contributors to the cause of hockey in WA.

In the late eighties came Alan Grant-Smith, who brought a professional approach to everything he did. Into the nineties came Ian Pitt and Neil Mannolini. These two ran the WA Hockey Stadium and Hockey Bulletin with great energy and made them the envy of other States. Ralph Wood was appointed CEO after the demise of Alan Grant-Smith.

Alan Grant-Smith was a person with eminent organizational ability. One of his pet projects was to organize from Perth an international Asian Hockey League. I arranged contacts with Asian hockey officials who had been my old friends in India. Alan put together beautifully bound colour proposals outlining his concept.

Briefly, the idea was to play televised games between Pakistan, India, Australia (WA) and Malaysia on a round-robin basis. The whole project was a brand new concept, which was hopefully going to be sold to a pay-television group whose programmes were beamed into South-East Asia from their base in Hong Kong.

Alan and I set off for meetings in Calcutta, New Delhi and the headquarters of the Indian Hockey Federation. All three Associations agreed with the concept without hesitation, because the funding was not to be carried by them, and it would expose their National teams to more international games than they could otherwise afford.

The synthetic hockey grounds at Calcutta and New Delhi were made-for-television venues, provided we got the cooperation of the local Hockey Associations.

Unfortunately the whole project had to be abandoned

because the world hockey governing body FIH signed a contract separately for *all* Hockey Internationals, which put paid to our Asian League.

Alan Grant Smith was a very disappointed man. Not long after that he resigned his position as CEO of the WA Hockey Association. He was always dedicated to 'due process' and this put him offside with well-meaning but impatient honorary members of various committees he chaired. In the end Alan walked away and WA lost a good man. Alan was a gentleman of great ability and it was felt by reasonable people that he had done the Association proud in his years at the helm.

1970'S IN WEST AUSTRALIA

While I do not profess to have completely coached the list of players below to their ultimate selection to Senior International Status, I feel I had started a mind set with each of them when in their impressionable teenage years and convinced them that they were good enough to go all the way with this their chosen sport, if they kept improving. They did!

Players that were coached when young by me, Trevor Vanderputt, who went on to be Internationals and Senior Club coaches in Western Australia included:

PETER HASELHURST

CRICKETERS H. C. /WA STATE U/16 AND U/21/ WA SENIORS/AUSTRALIA

Peter and his brother Geoff both starred in WA State Junior teams coached by me: 1973 (Canberra) – undefeated champions; 1975 (Hobart) – second (Geoff). Peter was then selected for WA Colts (U/21) in 1976 (Adelaide). Lost in sudden death semi-final. Peter was the most stick-skilled Australian born player in the mould of that great Indian,

'Babu'. One of Australia's greatest forwards, he burst on the Seniors scene during the Cricketers Hockey Club tour of India in 1978, with the great Ric Charlesworth as his skipper. His mentors included Bob Andrew, Charlesworth and Dick Aggiss.

CRAIG DAVIES

OLD AQUINIANS/CRICKETERS H.C./WA STATE U/16,U/21,SENIORS, /AUSTRALIA

Son of the famed Aussie Rules Sandover Medal winner Jim Davies, Craig decided he wanted to play hockey and not football. The most outstanding junior in Australia, he rapidly rose from Juniors to Colts to Senior level in WA. It was no surprise to anyone when Craig was selected to the Australian National Senior Squad. He performed with skill, courage and leadership qualities to finally be named Captain after Charlesworth stepped down. His strong points were penalty corner hitting, strong tackling, and beautiful passing of the ball out of defence. Latterly he tried his hand at coaching and playing for the Fremantle Hockey Club. It was sad to read a few years ago that he suffered from an unusual heart complaint! This was a complete surprise to all, as Craig was such a physical fitness fanatic all his life to that stage. Married to his long-time sweetheart, with two lovely sons, Craig can be seen training and coaching them at his beloved sport. He went on to be Head Coach and Administrator of the WA Institute of Sport.

TERRY LEESE

PERTH YMCA HOCKEY CLUB, /WA STATE U/16, U/21, SENIORS/AUSTRALIA

As a very young 13 year-old Terry was the best kid on the field for his beloved YMCA team. His was a Club that produced Don Smart, Don Martin, David Hatt, Brian Glencross, Mike O'Reilly, the Boyce brothers and Terry Walsh, all champions of that era (the seventies). With this as his pedigree in coaching and mixing with successful players, Terry progressed to the State sides with Haselhurst and Davies, eventually graduating to the Australian team. Lovely stick skills, ball control, and the ability to eliminate defenders with ease, Terry Leese was a delight to watch. He went on to coach YMCA at the highest level after a stint with Fremantle Hockey Club.

STEVE HAYWARD

GERALDTON/UNIVERSITY/STATE COLTS/ SENIORS/ AUSTRALIA

From a country town north of Perth in WA, Steve was a tough, no-nonsense full-back who was quick (unusual for a full back), a great tackler, and a wonderful talent at scoring from penalty corners. Because he was a 'typical country-style' player he was considered a rough defender and was nicknamed Doc (because he fixed them up!)

Steve captained my Colts team in 1976 and was added to the Cricketers India Tour squad because Craig Davies could not make the trip. He was superb! A rock of a full-back, he wowed the Indian hockey fans. Won the inaugural WA Olympians Medal for Best and Fairest 1A Player. It was no surprise that he was selected for Australia. Latterly Doc played for the South Perth Hockey Club, which became WASPS or Wesley South Perth. Still plays Vets' Hockey and loves the game with a passion. Was a very good friend of future Australian coach Frank Murray. John Goldie was his Colts coach before I took over the job. Aggiss and Murray had a lot to do with his later development.

GRANT BOYCE

PERTH YMCA/STATE U/16/U21, SENIORS & AUSTRALIA

Another fine YMCA product who, along with elder brother Craig, was the backbone of the WA State Senior sides of the seventies and early eighties. Rarely did Grant miss a trap from an early age. Very well balanced, he could feed his forwards with a stream of passes, and was also a reliable defender. He was at first the understudy to the great David Bell, who had a mortgage on the right-half position, and then a ready replacement when David Bell moved to centre-half for the State Seniors. He also replaced Bell when the latter was injured at the LA Olympics. Very cool and a fine half-back. Grant went on to coach YMCA teams.

JAY STACEY

CAMBERWELL H/C STATE U/14, U/16, U/21/ SENIORS/AUSTRALIA

Jay played for me in the 1981 Australian Junior Championships. I played him as a half-back and he was outstanding. After being admitted to the Australian Institute of Sport Hockey Unit in Perth under master coach Dick Aggiss, Jay went on to be one of the top forwards of the Australian teams in the eighties. Big and strong, a powerful penalty corner hitter. Was moved to the forward line as a right inner mid-fielder who played rather deep and gave long 'killer' passes. This was, in my opinion, a wrong tactic and even though Australia won many an International with Jay working behind the play, I still felt he was too slow to be a fully effective Inside Right. A very outspoken player who was finally dropped from the Australian Squad and the Vice-Captaincy. Victorian Coach Jim Irvine had a lot to do with Jay Stacey in his early development, and Frank Murray was always his biggest supporter in the years he was in Frank's Australian sides.

LACHLAN DREHER

T. E. M'S (MELBOURNE) STATE U/14, U/16, COLTS AND SENIORS/AUSTRALIA

'Lockie' was a splendid goalkeeper and played for Australia for many a year. Very cool under pressure and a Coach's dream as a team man. Another product of Aggiss' AIS coaching. Kept his spot in the National team in spite of very strong competition from very good goalkeepers, and shared the position with WA's Damon Delletti in the nineties. A very likeable man, who in my opinion should be made captain of the National team (2001.) This is how highly I rate Lachlan Dreher! One of Victoria's best.

ANDREW DEAN

CANBERRA ST. PATS H. C. U/16, COLTS, SENIORS (ACT) /AUSTRALIA

Andrew is the son of ex-NSW Senior player Terry Dean. Was coached in Colts by Bob Taylor (also a NSW Player). Andrew was a very fast-running Right Wing or Centre Forward with good control and shot on goal. He caught the eye of the selectors and was invited to join the AIS in Perth. Aggiss soon found him good enough to play for Australia, much to the delight of his home State, Australian Capital Territory, that had also produced Olympian Errol Bill for the 1960 Olympic team at Rome.

GREGORY CORBITT

PERTH SUBURBAN/STATE U/16/COLTS/SENIORS/AUSTRALIA

Greg is the son of Don Corbitt, a senior player with the old Suburban Club, one of the oldest hockey clubs in Perth. A very talented player, a product of the West Australian juniors, I invited Greg to tour with the WA Combined Invitation Team in 1986, to play in New Delhi at the All-India Sardar Mohan Singh Hockey Tournament at the Shivaji Stadium. This fine stadium was the old Lady Harding Ground during the author's heyday in New Delhi in the early fifties.

Very strong on the ball, with a powerful hit, a devastating flick and a wonderful shot on goal, Greg was so impressive that veteran hockey umpire, coach and author Sardar Gian Singh commented that this was a player with a very rare talent, even though Greg was only 16 at the time. It was predicted by both Gian and the author that Greg would go on to play for Australia. Aggiss was also impressed with Greg's play and he soon joined the AIS. The rest is history. A serious injury ended Corbitt's International hockey career and though he tried a comeback after two years out of the game he never succeeded in regaining selection. A great pity, as Greg was a wonderful prospect to play for many more years for Australia.

RICHARD (DICK) AGGISS

OLD MODERNIANS H. C. /AQUINIANS H. C

'Dodger' is the name Richard acquired while on a tour of Malaysia with the West Australian team, according to Mal Poole who was also on the team. Dodger hailed from Harvey, near the town of Bunbury in the south of Western Australia He moved to Albany in 1962. While studying in

Perth for his teacher's degree he played hockey under legendary coach Merv Adams. He was a powerfully built, strong, hard hitting full-back who caught the eye of the State selectors, and first played in 1969 for the then powerful West Australian hockey State side. He played alongside the great Brian Glencross and Laurie (the Mongrel) Bedford. Dick dominated the position for ten long years 1969-1978.

When Merv Adams became the Australian Coach Richard took over the WA State coaching job. He had moved from Mods to Aquinas to try his hand at coaching, and won a Premiership for Aquinas in 1974. Aggiss had a great influence on the young players of that remarkable era, such as Ric Charlesworth, David Bell, Terry Walsh, the Boyce brothers (Craig and Grant), Craig Davies, Peter Haselhurst, Terry Leese, Steve Smith and Steve Hayward. All went on to represent Australia at the highest level.

Aggiss came into his own as a Master Coach when he was appointed Australian Coach in 1981. His record is as follows:

COACHING RECORD

Coached 151 Internationals to Nov 1988. Won 103, drew 25, lost 23

Head Coach Australian Institute of Sport (Hockey Division) 1984 -94

Australian Coach			1981-1988
Champions Tournament	Trophy	2nd	1982 Amsterdam
World Cup		3rd	1982 Bombay
Champions Tournament	Trophy	Gold Medal	1983 Karachi

Champions Tournament	Trophy	Gold Medal	1984 Karachi
Olympic Games		4th	1984 LA
Champions Tournament	Trophy	Gold Medal	1985 Perth
World Cup		Gold Medal	1986 London
Champions Tournament	Trophy	2nd	1986 Karachi
Champions Tournament	Trophy	3rd	1987 Amsterdam
Olympic Games		4th	1988 Seoul
Champions Tournament	Trophy	3rd	1988 Pakistan

PLAYING RECORD

WA State Hockey Team   1969,70,71 and 74

Australian National Team

National highlights include 1st. World Cup Spain. 1971. Also played against New Zealand, Japan, Pakistan and Holland.

AWARDS

1988	Order of Australia A. M. for Services to Hockey.
1987	Sport Australia Award-Coach Of the Year
1987	WA R&I Coach of the Year
1984	FIH World Coach

The record of Richard Aggiss speaks for itself, but what it does not spell out is the nature of the man, and his never-failing support for the cause of hockey. Some examples:

When I was Director of Coaching for the ACT Hockey Association in Canberra I initiated a Level 2 Coaching Course (see Chapter Six.) Dick was kind enough to give up a full weekend, flying from Perth to Canberra to help his friend run the Course and give it some strong backing. Thanks, Richard. You did a wonderful job!

When a certain Clary Miller approached Dick to get his support for the book Clary was writing, Dick not only gave Clary many hours of his time and experience in completing the book, he was also instrumental in getting Esanda Finance, at the time hockey's main Sponsor in Australia, to fund the printing of the book, much to Clary Miller's delight. In this he was wonderfully supported by Merv Potter, the WA State Manager, and Sales Manager Eric Pearce.

While I did not agree with some of Dick's player selections, I must concede that 90% of the time he was correct in his judgment of players' capabilities. His record more than proves this.

The players he pulled from obscurity in my humble opinion were: Neil Hawgood, Grant Mitton, Dean Evans (although Frank Murray had a lot to do with this selection as well), Mark Hager, Kenny Wark, Warren Birmingham, Treva King and John Bestall. All made a wonderful contribution to Dick Aggiss's winning teams and made Australia a team to be feared in the eighties.

Richard Aggiss learnt a lot from Merv Adams, and in turn passed on to his successor Frank Murray the rudiments of coaching at the highest level. Frank had his detractors, and I was one to sometimes question his judgement in the matter of playing certain players year after year when they were not producing the goods and had obviously long passed their use-by date. Nevertheless, Frank Murray had an enviable coaching record. To his bitter disappointment, however, just like Aggiss and Adams before him and Terry Walsh who followed him in the job, all failed to win a Gold Medal at the Olympics with the men. Some of them, like Glencross and Frank Murray, turned to coaching the Australian Women's team and won Gold Medals with the women at Seoul (Glencross) and Sydney (Murray, as assistant Coach to Charlesworth).

ROBERT (THE COLONEL) ANDREW

CRICKETERS H.C./WA JUNIORS/SENIORS, AUSTRALIA

Bob Andrew starred in his early hockey days as a forward. He was selected for the Australian Hockey team when Charlie Morley the Victorian was the National Coach, but did not get many opportunities even though he was in the squad. In his position were such great players as Pat Nilan and Des Piper, so the young Andrew sat on the bench for most of his early stint as an Australian player.

It was in the National Championships held in Perth in 1970 that the WA Coach Merv Adams developed Bob into the half-back line and Bob played so well that he was selected as right half-back in the National team and went to the Munich Olympics in 1972.

When Bob returned from the Olympic Games, and Sharpe, the Cricketers' regular centre-half, moved to Bunbury, Bob moved to centre half-back and excelled in this position. Being Captain/Coach as well as centre-half of Perth's best hockey team was a task 'The Colonel' performed admirably. And all this time he had to handle the likes of Ric Charlesworth and young rising star Peter Haselhurst. One of them (Charlie) loved training and the other (Peter) hated the bloody time training! Despite this,

Bob Andrew remains one of the great players produced by Western Australia in the sixties and seventies. A real ornament to the game of hockey!

BRIAN GLENCROSS

(YMCA) WEST AUSTRALIA/AUSTRALIAN OLYMPIAN 1964-1968-1972 (CAPTAIN)

'Bags', as Brian was called, was a superb full-back – in my opinion the best full-back in the classical mould. Skilful in play, positioning and tackling. Impeccable in disposal and cover defence. A fine penalty corner hitter before the rules precluded lifted shots on goal from first strikes on penalty corners When his playing days were over Brian turned to coaching. Richard Aggiss and Brian Glencross were appointed as the first two full-time Head Coaches of the newly-formed Australian Institute of Sport's Hockey Programme in Perth. This led to Brian taking the Australian Women's team to Seoul for the Olympics. With Peter Freitag as his assistant the team won the coveted Gold Medal for the first time.

Brian, himself, had been coached as a young kid at the YMCA Club in Perth by the great Anglo-Indian Bengal and BNR full-back Ivan 'Honey' Meade. Ivan, who hailed from Kharagpur, a small Railway town not far from Calcutta, also had the record of coaching Indian legend Leslie Claudius when Claudius was only 16. Claudius himself was an Anglo-Indian from another Indian Railway town called Bilaspur. Thus Ivan has the unique distinction of having coached both the captain of India, Claudius (1960) and the captain of Australia, Glencross (1972).

TERRY WALSH

*YMCA PERTH/STATE JUNIORS/SENIORS
AUSTRALIA*

This amazing player and later coach was the son of ex-Rawalpindi Anglo-Indian John Walsh. Terry and his younger brother Peter spent some time as youngsters in the Goldfield town of Kalgoorlie, where their father was the Principal of the local school. On John Walsh's transfer back to Perth the Walsh boys played and learnt their craft at the strong YMCA Club that boasted the Glencross brothers, Don Smart, the Martin brothers, Mike O'Reilly and many other famous WA players. It was under John Goldie and in the company of Charlesworth, Craig and Grant Boyce that Terry was noticed, along with David Bell (Aquinians) in the WA Colts teams of the early seventies by the Australian selectors. Bell and Terry Walsh were picked in the Australian side of 1974. Within two years both Bell and Terry were in the Olympic team for Montreal. Terry was a dashing striker who had played earlier as a left-winger and later as a centre-forward. He damaged his knee and always played thereafter with his knee very heavily strapped. A lot of defenders wrongly assumed that this was going to slow Terry Walsh down. On the contrary, he seemed to travel and try that much harder. Scoring with monotonous frequency, he was the most feared forward in the Australian attack. Terry Walsh, along with the great Charlesworth and Mal Poole, formed a wonderful combination at Montreal. The team won the Silver Medal there and went on to win the Gold Medal at the World Cup in 1986 in London.

Terry Walsh was appointed Assistant Coach under Richard Aggiss at the AIS and did a stint in Malaysia as that country's National Coach in 1990. On his return to Perth a few years later he was appointed National Men's Coach when Frank Murray gave up the job. Terry was a very disappointed man when Australia failed to win the coveted Gold Medal at the Sydney Olympics. He was replaced by Queenslander Barry Dancer as Head Coach of the National team after the Sydney Games.

MIKE NOBBS

SOUTH AUSTRALIA- SUBURBAN H.C. PERTH, UNI OF WA, HALE SCHOOL/ TRINITY THUNDERSTICKS AND AUSTRALIA (OLYMPICS 1984)

According to retired Australian National Umpire Ian Pitt who hailed from Adelaide, South Australia, Mike Nobbs as a kid learned his hockey from Anglo-Indian migrants in Adelaide. This accounted for his magnificent Indian-style stick work and love of the game.

His name was first mentioned by John Goldie, the WA Colts coach, on his return from a Colts Championship in the early 1970's. When asked which Colts players from the Championship were the most outstanding, Goldie replied: 'Charlesworth and Nobbs.' Nobbs was outstanding at full-back playing alongside Don Prior and went on to play State Seniors hockey. Prior went on to be an outstanding International Umpire.

Mike Nobbs had it all as a player! He was tall, athletic, strong on the ball, a good hockey brain, wonderful stick work, a fine overhead flick and a sound reader of the play. His only weakness, if he had one, was, in my opinion, a not very strong hit out of defence. This, I suppose, was the reason his National Coach played him as a half-back, where his push passes and all-round game became apparent and made him into one of the best centre-halves in Australia in the eighties and nineties.

By the eighties Mike moved his residence to Perth from Adelaide. He was snapped up by the 'Rent-A-Team'

Suburban Hockey Club. He helped win three Perth Premierships on the trot and then moved on to coach for the first time, with the University of WA. Playing at centre-half, coaching and being captain at the same time, he took the Uni team to four Grand Finals. At 40 years of age, and arguably the best centre-half in West Australia, Mike took on the new challenge of coaching Hale School, newly-promoted to 1A's. He stayed with them three years, during which time he was appointed State Team coach of the Thundersticks and won two Australian Championships.

Mike's exposure to the West flowed on to Women's coaching as well. After a long courtship he married Lee Capes, a dynamic Australian Olympic right-winger who won a Gold Medal at the Seoul Olympics in 1988. Lee's mother June Haines and Aunt Shirley Haines were both Australian Internationals, as was her sister Michelle Capes, a dual Olympic Gold Medal winner. Michelle married Australian ace centre-forward Mark Hager.

So all in all a whole lot of good hockey genes in these bloodlines!

I knew and supported Mike Nobbs because I hired him as a sales executive for my firm Gestetner. He was successful, but the lure of hockey coaching was in his blood. He was appointed to a coaching position in Japan. For nine years during the off-season in Perth he returned to coach there, winning for his University-based team two All-Japan titles and seven Inter-Collegiate titles.

When news from India indicated they were exploring the possibility of appointing a 'foreign' National Coach, I suggested that Mike apply for the position. I put his name up to some old friends still active in Indian Hockey affairs in Calcutta and New Delhi, who tried to have him appointed. In the end, however, India decided to stick with one of their own. Mike was bitterly disappointed at missing out. I suspect the prospect of paying an Australian the kind of money that would attract a suitable candidate was beyond the Indian officials, so they stuck to the old formula and appointed a local.

Mike's plans for 2002 are to assist the Australian National Coach, Barry Dancer, with Advanced Skills Coaching for the National Squad of players. With Barry at the helm and assistants as good as Colin Batch and Mike Nobbs to help, the Australians must be a better team to contend with in the foreseeable future.

My last word on Mike Nobbs: a soft-spoken, pleasant motivator, a good husband and dad to two lovely future junior champions, a credit to the game of hockey, and above all a good friend and a gentleman!

OTHER NOTABLE WEST AUSTRALIANS

Peter Shepherd (Trinity and Old Aquinians) was one of the best goalkeepers that, due to playing in the strong WA team, never shone at National Championships and was thus never recognized or selected to play for Australia.

Other good keepers at that time were Dick (Speedy) Osbourne (Cricketers H.C.), John Nettleton (Uni), Glen Carlson (Cricketers) and Hodgens (YMCA).

Don 'The Great' Barker (Perth): A wonderful right-half who finally gave up his position to a young David Bell, who went on to captain Australia in their World Cup win in 1986, to add to his Olympic Silver Medal (1976).

David Bell, son of another fine player of the fifties (Ian Bell) was the closest to India's Leslie Claudius the author has seen. That is the highest praise one could heap on a right-half.

Ian Biddle (Old Mods): A centre-half, second only to the great Julian Pearce who dominated this position in the early seventies.

David Hatt (YMCA) a sound, polished centre-half and disciplined player, was a Merv Adams selection, and went on to win three Australian Championships with the WA state seniors.

Steven Smith (Old Mods/Old Aquinians): another Adam's protégé who was singled out early and went on to play for Australia. A sparkling left-winger with speed and dash – a necessity for any good side.

Malcolm Poole (South Perth): a fine forward with good stick skills. Played inside-left, with Terry Walsh on his left and Charlesworth at inside-right. Won a Silver Medal at Montreal in 1976.

Don and Peter Martin, young migrants from Malaysia, soon made a name for themselves in Perth hockey. Don was selected to play in the 1964 and 1968 Olympics at right-wing and won a Silver and a Bronze Medal. Fine stick skills together with good speed on the wing. Don Martin gave good value to this very talented team. In that same team were fellow YMCA stalwarts for many years, Don Smart and brilliant full-back Brian Glencross.

Don Smart is the son of an Anglo-Indian. Don was born in Burma and came to Australia as a very young lad. His Dad had played for the Calcutta Rangers club and was an astute judge of the game. Don had all the skills, and in my opinion was the Australian with stick skills to match any Indian or Pakistani player. He could play either left-wing or inside-left with equal skill. Went on to play and coach South Perth when they made the First Division in 1970. He was the first coach to try tactics different to the popular Indian Orthodox 5:3:2:1 formation. Don played in the 1964, 1968 and 1972 Olympics and played well. Later he made a name for himself as a coach of the WA Colts (U/21) and Australian U/21 teams. A wonderful contributor to the game!

FLASHBACK:

AUSTRALIAN HOCKEY IN THE THIRTIES

One of the more talented players to come to Australia from India in the 30's was a Dennis Dunbar. He migrated to Adelaide and played hockey there before moving to Perth and playing for the Suburban Hockey Club. He had originally played for the Calcutta Rangers Club and had taught hockey as a Sports Master in his old school, Saint Paul's, Darjeeling. He finished top goal-scorer in the WA league before moving to the University Hockey Club, where he coached the top side that included Syd Johnson.

Other strong Clubs then were Suburban, Perth, Cricketers' and Guildford. George Milner was the outstanding player of this era.

The Second World War stopped all competitions, so it was a quiet period for hockey and other sports. In 1946 there was a revival, including an Australian Hockey Carnival. The shock of the 1946 Carnival was the non-attendance of the NSW team.

The WA team captain in this year was A. J. Prosser from Cricketers Club. Prosser had earlier played for Australia. The vice-captain was E. Southwood from Uni H.C., back from the war where he had served in the Army. Southwood was a penalty corner expert. Tall and powerfully built, he was the scourge of goalkeepers Laurie Bandy and the Dick brothers (all Cricketers players). It was at this tourney that Ian Dick stood out as a neat, balanced beautiful passer of the ball and predictions were made that he would not only play for Australia but would also one day be Captain. Danny Dunn was a 22 year-old playing centre-half and handled the ball well. Danny was from the Uni H.C. and was eventually made a Life Member.

The list is too numerous to identify in full all the great

players of this era. The Vics had legend Charley Morley and also a very young Keith Thornton, both from the Camberwell Hockey Club, which was a top Club in Melbourne and still is. Their efforts and accomplishments were many. However, the difference in class between Australia and India in 1935/6 can be clearly seen from the following account.

In 1938 an Indian princely state, Manavada, sent a hockey team to tour New Zealand and Australia. The Australian game scheduled for Perth was looked forward to with great interest. The captain of the WA team was George Milner from the Perth Hockey Club. The centre-forward selected for that historic match was University's Syd Johnson. Other notable players were Cricketers' Doug and Eric McKenzie. The Manavada team boasted three Indian senior internationals. They were Mohammed Hussain, Shahabuddin and Peter Fernandes. All three were in the victorious Indian Olympic team that had won the Gold Medal at the Berlin Games in 1936. Despite the efforts of the West Australians including Syd Johnson, this was the sad outcome:

RESULTS OF THE INDIAN TOURING TEAM

Beat WA at Perth	11-2
Beat SA	10-1
Beat Victoria	15-1
Beat Sydney	11-4
Beat NSW in Sydney	11-0
Beat ACT in Canberra	12-1
Beat Australia in Melb.	12-0
Beat WA at Perth	16-0

All this began to change significantly when the Anglo-Indians started to arrive after the British left India in mid-1947.

The Anglo-Indians were Indian by domicile but were in

fact of European stock. They were the masters of the game of hockey. Their influence soon changed the style of the game and system of play here, and laid the foundation of Australia's eminent position in world hockey that prevails today.

WA HOCKEY IN THE THIRTIES AND FORTIES

A group of WA State and Club cricket players decided they wanted to play hockey together in the winter months to keep fitness levels up to scratch and also enjoy one another's company. The brothers Eric and Doug McKenzie were the main instigators in the founding of Cricketers Hockey Club. The early name was Claremont Cricketers Club because most of the gang were members of the Claremont Cricket team and lived in the Claremont area of Perth.

A leading Aussie Rules League player and a star was Johnny Leonard. He played right wing. Also starring at the time in the Perth Hockey League was the University of Western Australia's Harry Hopkins, the captain. Don Tregonning was a splendid player of the time and was selected to play for the Australian National team to play New Zealand in the Manning Cup to be held in Sydney. His untimely death in 1935 while on his way with the State team to the East was a great shock and a huge loss to Australian and West Australian hockey.

George Milner of the Perth H.C. was Captain of the State in 1936. Vice-Captain was Doug McKenzie. A leading goal-getter from the University H.C. was Syd Johnson. In that side dominated with Cricketers' players were Taaffe, Doug and Eric McKenzie, Prosser, Bandy and Hall.

In 1938, the Carnival (that's what Interstate Championships were called) was held in Adelaide. H.R. Bickford was the Captain and his team was a strong one, comprising R. Truscott (Vice-Captain), Tom Bedells (later to be a top umpire), D. Allnut, L. Angel, L. Bandy, E.

Ellershaw, J.L. Gorn, G. Griffith, R. Jones, B. St. J. Kennedy, T. Lalor, G. Mattiske, E. Southwood, R. Warren and A.J. Todd.

State Captains for that Carnival were as follows:
South Australia: J.L. Allen (H. F. Bowden in the side.)
Queensland: J. Mahoney (Hec Cormie Manager)
N.S.W. Jack Prosser (Ex-Perth player and L. Felsch)
Victoria (Finley McNabb and Charlie Morley)
Tasmania: L. Dalglish (A. Addison).

In the 1950's the Anglo-Indians' influence on the hockey scene in Perth started to take effect with Fred Browne, Cyril Carton, Ivan Meade, Derek Munrowd, Merv Adams and the Pearce Brothers. The WA State sides, with Ian Dick, Alan Barblett, Gren Davies, Peter Kennedy and Bob Hancock, among others, were so strong that at one Carnival they had No Goals Against. The Goalkeeper then was Vern Gooch. To this day he reminds those that want to hear of yesteryear that his record can never be beaten, only equalled! Well done, Vern!

These trips East were always by train, and on occasions the train stopped on the Nullarbor to take on water and coal. The lads would pull out their hockey sticks and have a training hit during such stops in the middle of nowhere!

The 1956 Olympic Games in Melbourne saw Ian Dick elected as Captain. Alan Barblett, Des Spackman, Kevin Carton, Keith Leeson, Dennis Kemp, Raymond Whiteside, Melville, Eric and Gordon Pearce, Maurice Foley were some of the players, and Fred Browne was the coach. Australia came fifth in their first appearance at the Olympics. India beat Pakistan in the final.

In the early 1960's India held an international tourney in the city of Ahmedabad. Australia sent a team which was a revelation to the hockey fraternity. One of the umpires at this tourney was an Indian by the name of Santosh

Gangulie who hailed from Calcutta. He came over to the Calcutta Rangers Club Tent on the hockey oval and gave some of the members who were there, including me, a bit of a talk on the standard of the players from overseas. 'Watch out for the Australians,' said Santosh (after his third Scotch and soda.) 'They play hockey like the Anglo-Indians of the golden days of the thirties and will be a threat to all sides from now on.'

How right was he? Bronze at Tokyo in 1964, silver at Mexico in 1968, silver at Montreal in 1976! Later, under Richard Aggiss, numerous gold Champions trophies, and in 1986, World Cup Gold! Australian Hockey had come of age, and some degree of credit must surely be given to the Anglo-Indians.

SYD JOHNSON

In 1936 Syd was selected to represent WA University at the All-Australian University Games in Sydney. After the Games Syd was selected in the All-Australian University team as Captain. According to Syd, his hero, guide and mentor was that great player Harry Hopkins. One of Syd's great games was the Challenge Cup Final of 1938, when Uni defeated Cricketers 3-2. Another notable game was Uni versus Fremantle in the A-1 grade when Syd Johnson was in tremendous form and scored FIVE goals in his team's win of 8-5. Uni was undoubtedly one of the best sides in the late thirties. The facilities they had far outstripped the other Clubs and they thus attracted the cream of the private schools that went on to tertiary studies.

Syd Johnson, like so many others, joined up during the War and served in the Pathfinder Squadron in the RAF where he was decorated for his missions over war-torn Europe. After the War Syd was again selected to represent WA, in 1946 and 1947.

Syd Johnson was a member of the WA State Senior side

from 1936 to 1947, except for the War years.

In 1948 Syd was made Vice-President of the West Australian Hockey Association and the following year, 1949, he went to Papua New Guinea for the Crown Law Department, where he served for twenty years. To honour him for his contribution to WA hockey, Syd was made a Life Member of the Association.

MERV ADAMS

In 1953 Merv accepted an invitation from the late Colin Campbell who was then Secretary of the Old Modernians Hockey Club, to come down, have a run and perhaps offer a few tips to the players. The stay at 'Mods' was to be a long one and by the late 1960's he had developed a group of juniors into one of the top A grade Clubs in Perth.

The inevitable happened. Merv Adams was elected State Senior Coach in 1964 and the old master's star began to shine brightly once again. Eight Australian Championships in 10 years at the helm, a feat that has never been achieved before, and is unlikely to happen again. The crowning glory of his State team was in 1964 when WA defeated World Champions Pakistan at Perry Lakes Stadium. Merv was duly selected to take over the National team's coaching position after the debacle in Munich in 1972. On his appointment to the job in 1973 he immediately set about preparing his squad for the Montreal Olympics in 1976, mostly by correspondence. It is written into hockey's history books that Australia had to settle for a Silver Medal after having beaten the World's best, only to lose surprisingly to New Zealand in the play-off for the Gold Medal.

In 1978 Japan invited Merv to assist in the coaching of their National team. Later that year the Australian Women's Hockey Association appointed Merv to coach the Women's National team in an endeavour to gain a birth at the

Moscow Olympics. This was achieved for the first time ever when Australia finished fourth at a classification tournament held at Vancouver, Canada. Adams was clearly the spark that was lit for the Aussie Hockey teams, both Men and Women, to reach the dizzy heights. Both teams, since his demise, have reached the Top. The Men's Team achieved a World Cup and many Champions Trophy Wins; and the Women's team became Olympic Champions in three out of the last four Olympics.

Merv Adams had a great deal to do with the development of many players in Australia. He was a great supporter of Ray Evans and Ian Biddle. He picked out Mal Poole when he was a Colt. He nurtured Steven Smith when he was just 14 years old, and always said his star full-backs in the 70's were Brian Glencross and Dick Aggiss, with Laurie Bedford as his 'Third Back' Merv guided Bob Andrew into the half-back line and was always of the opinion that Julian Pearce and his brother Gordon were two that would have starred in any era.

Some of Merv's thoughts as told to the author Trevor Vanderputt were:

Greatest skilled player of his time in Australia:	Don Smart
Best All-Round Hockey player To represent Australia:	Richard Charlesworth
Best Goal Scorer of the time:	Eric Pearce
Best Junior of his time:	David Bell
Best reader of the play:	Dick Aggis & Frank Murray
Hardest 'Worker':	Terry Walsh
His 'Idol':	Indian Captain (1952) K.D. Singh 'Babu'

Merv Adams was a quiet, humble man with a ready smile and a chuckle, totally dedicated to the sport he loved, giving, always giving, setting an example that others followed not just for themselves, but for the Sport.

The great strides forward for hockey in Australia, together with the glittering future Merv predicted, in no small way lives as a monument to Merv Adams.

(*Special Note: Most of this section on Merv Adams was taken from an 'Old Aquinas Tribute' by Ted Pitts.*)

The following is from an article written by the author when he was Director of Coaching in Canberra:

'BALDY': MY MATE AND MENTOR

CANBERRA – 15 DECEMBER 1981

Here in Canberra Merv Adams had made a lot of friends as he had come from Perth to Coach on more than one occasion. Merv, like myself hailed from India so we spoke the same Hockey Language. Always smiling and using his special kind of humour his company was a delight to those who came in contact with him.

After the Olympics at Montreal Merv was a bitterly disappointed man in winning a Silver Medal when a Gold was oh so close. He and his Manager, Keith Murton, both returned to Australia to face the Hockey public who thought winning Silver (as opposed to Gold) was a failure! He was relieved of the Coaching position and some time later was appointed National Coach of the Women in 1979.

On what turned out to be his last hockey tour he coached the Women to a fine performance in Vancouver Canada. This qualified them to be included in future Olympic Games for the first time ever. It was in Vancouver that Merv suffered a heart attack. Colin Nicholas the President of the W A Hockey Association at the time, on receiving the news, used his initiative and got Merv's wife

Peggy on a plane to Canada to be by her husband's bedside in his final hours. Merv passed away a week later and at his memorial service in Claremont, Western Australia, the Hockey fraternity turned out in force to pay a final tribute to this great Hockey stalwart, the like of which will never be seen again.

'Rest in Peace' Baldy, it was nice knowing you.

CHAPTER SIX: *Melbourne Memories*

In the state of Victoria, Melbourne's Camberwell Hockey Club was at the forefront of the State's contribution to Australian hockey. It produced players and coaches par excellence. The Victorian Hockey Association was fortunate to have people and players so involved with the State's hockey aspirations.

Charley Morley would arguably be the greatest influence on Victorian and Australian hockey in the immediate post-World War 2 period. It was Charlie who started to think outside the circle and experiment with team field positions. The acknowledged masters of the game till then, the Indians, used the orthodox field placings: five forwards, three half-backs, two full-backs and a goalkeeper. They had won six Olympic Gold Medals using this system.

The end of the British Raj in India saw a massive influx of Anglo-Indians into Australia from 1947 onwards. Most of these players settled in Western Australia. Here they continued to play and teach the orthodox 5:3:2:1 style of teamwork, and proved too strong for the other States. Although some of the other State teams did play the orthodox style as well, they were not able to master the techniques taught by Cyril Carton, Ivan Meade, Fred Browne in the past, and more recently by Merv Adams with senior players and Trevor Vanderputt with juniors.

Charley Morley also tried the 'Possession' game as implemented in Europe with players in teams under him. Indoor Hockey was another initiative Charlie Morley was responsible for. Morley in his time was, at one stage or another, Captain, Selector, Coach, Manager and lastly

Secretary of the Australian Hockey Association. He was undoubtedly Victoria's greatest contributor to Australian hockey for over twenty years.

Mike Craig, who was Captain in Rome, Keith Thornton and Graham Wood, all from the Camberwell Club, carried on the strong tradition of the Club at international level. This club finished Premiers of Victoria in 1932 and 1935, 1938 and 1940.

After the war the club won six premierships in a row (1946-51), then between 1952 and 1965 they won another four Premierships and were never lower than third during this period. What a record! Charlie Morley must have been one hell of a coach.

Some of the greatest Camberwell Club and Victorian State players were: Colin Wansbrough, Ric Purser, Arthur Reid, Doug Stewart, Bill Horman and Alan Carnell. With this great record the Vics were always of the mind that they were kings of Australian hockey. Consequently they assumed that with all this talent they had in Victoria, a Victorian coach should take charge of the National team. Sure enough, with Charlie Morley there to push the Victorian barrow, Arthur Sturgess was appointed Coach, much to the dismay of hockey people in the West.

Arthur was National Coach in 1968 and 1972. The Sturgess team that went to Mexico in 1968 was very strong. They were grand finalists, losing the final to Pakistan in a very rough game. In Munich the team was not quite as strong and the forwards were found wanting, apart from 'Sundance' Browning and a very young newcomer Ric Charlesworth. The defence was good except for the new centre-half but the team finished fifth and out of the finals. Australia had paid the price for Sturgess' stubborn decision to persevere with a Victorian centre-half, a key position in any hockey team. That was the end of Sturgess and a dent in Victoria's domination of the game.

However, the contribution of Victorians to hockey must be recognised. Des Piper, who was the best Victorian International at the time, was followed by Jim Irvine and Colin Batch. Earlier players were Robin Hodder, Wayne Thornton, David Wansbrough, Keith Stevens, Lachlan Dreher, Jay Stacey, Neil Snowden, Nigel Patmore and Bob McLellan.

On the coaching side for Camberwell, apart from the inimitable Charlie Morley there were Mike Craig, Alan Carnell, Don Argus, who coached the State League First Division team in 1980 and 1981, Don Cashmere, who was the under-sixteens coach for both his Club and Victoria, and myself, Trevor Vanderputt, who coached the State under-fourteens team.

Victoria had some powerful administrators in the late seventies and eighties, including Presidents Harry Nederveen and Peter Cohen and Executive Officers Kim Harrison (pictured above, facing camera) and Keith Murton (pictured below). Then came the Australian Hockey Association's first National Coaching Director Ivan Spedding. He took over three years to prepare a Coaching Manual, which was a fine piece of work and was well worth the wait!

Bert Batch was another wonderful coach who served on numerous Victorian hockey teams. His son Colin was a great player and is now the Assistant Head Coach to Barry Dancer at the prestigious Hockey Unit of the Australian Institute of Sport in Perth (2002). Denis Morgan was a superb CEO for the Vics for many a year.

In this imposing list of hockey personalities mention must be made of Ric Purser, who was considered to be very unlucky never to play for Australia. He took up coaching the game he played so well and eventually won the position of Head Coach of the USA's National team, earning big money, the like of which could never be earned in Australia coaching hockey. His sad death was totally unexpected and was a huge loss.

In summary, the 'Vics' of my day were tough, very competitive campaigners and have always made a great contribution to Australian hockey. However, before synthetic surfaces began to make a difference they were somewhat restricted with their stick skills because of their atrocious weather conditions and thus very heavy grounds.

MEMORY-SNIPPETS

Once while visiting Melbourne I went to see a local League match. Running along the sideline was a coach yelling instructions to his team to 'Take him out!' I asked the coach politely, 'Why are you asking your players to play rough?' His memorable reply was: 'Here in Victoria we play hard and we have hearts as big as footballs!'

Charlie Morley was such a stickler for discipline that he was known to phone players up on a Friday night before a Saturday game to see if they were obeying orders by staying home. Before the commencement of a game he would sometimes line his players up and tap them on the shins with his hockey stick to check if they had their shin guards on!

When I was in Camberwell in 1980 their ground was surfaced with ashes or cinders. It was a very even surface and the ball moved surprisingly fast and true. Visiting teams found it hard to beat Charlie Morley's Camberwell sides, who were used to playing on this surface, even international sides like Kenya and the Wanderers from India. Much experience was gained by the 'Wells in hosting these teams.

In January 1980 I took up my position as Assistant Branch Manager of Gestetner Ltd in Melbourne, and my family moved into a flat in Toorak. The closest ground to where we lived was the Camberwell Hockey Club.

I took my young son David down to this Club not

knowing that it was one of the best organised hockey clubs in Melbourne. Their Senior Coach was Don Argus (pictured above), an ex-Queensland State player and now a senior executive at the National Bank of Australia. In spite of his heavy responsibilities at his place of work, he found the time to do what he loved doing, that is, coaching hockey. He was very impressive at it too.

I had trained my son David as a goalkeeper, and he proved a godsend to the U/17 team as they did not have a regular keeper.

I offered my services as a junior coach at the club and was welcomed. After one season with them the Club put my name up for State U/14 coach and I was fortunate to gain the appointment with their backing. On my team (see photo on the next page) I recognised many future senior and international players, and they all fulfilled my expectations. Lachlan Dreher and Jay Stacey went on to play for their State and Australia. Steven Purcell and Robert Clarke went on to be State Seniors – all outstanding young men and dedicated hockey players.

Although it was a good team, we didn't win the Championships that year for two reasons. One was that the finals were played in Tasmania and the soggy ground did not suit our short-passing game. The other reason was that the team that did win (if I remember correctly) was the New South Wales team, coached by none other than my ex-Glebe team-mate, star International Kenny Wark Snr.

Two of my charges that impressed me most even at that young age were the keeper Lachlan Dreher, and all-rounder Jay Stacey. Lachlan used to come to training on his push-bike carrying his keeper's gear in a large cricket-gear bag on the back of his bike. Never late, always attentive to team talks and always willing to give his coach's suggestions a try, Jay Stacey used to come to Indoor Hockey with a variety of coloured T-shirts in his bag to try and get a game with any team that was short of players. He was so keen to play in any position, it was no surprise that he went on to represent Australia at Senior level for many years.

I am not claiming that I taught these guys all they know, but hasten to add that after they had played under me they made the Australian Institute of Sport. There, under Head Coach Dick Aggiss and Assistant Coach Terry Walsh they were turned into champions.

I followed the careers of my youthful players through the years, long after they had left my team, sharing their successes as well as their disappointments and frustrations. Sadly, some brilliant players never reached their zenith.

One of these was a lad named David Wansborough, the son of past great Colin Wansborough. Father and son were dyed-in-the-wool Camberwell players. David made the Australian team and played magnificently at centre-half. However, his coach kept playing him at either centre-forward or inside forward, because at that time Australia were short of class forwards. With late career injuries and frustration at not playing at his preferred position David eventually gave up playing internationals, much to the consternation of Melbourne hockey stalwarts.

Another Victorian player to feel great disappointment was Steve Purcell. This lad was top scorer at the Inter-State Nationals held in Perth, and his side won the tournament that year. At that time Frank Murray had taken over from Dick Aggiss. For some mysterious reason the Selectors and Frank refused to select him for the National team.

Special mention must be made of Colin Batch, the son of outstanding coach Bert Batch. Colin's best position was at inside-right but unfortunately for him, Australia had icon Ric Charlesworth playing in that position.

Let me conclude my Melbourne memories on a happier note, with a summary of the best from Victoria.

We remember from earlier times Mike Craig, Robin

Hodder and Des Piper. Craig captained the Australian team at the Rome Olympics. Des Piper was a Bronze and Silver medallist winner at Tokyo and Mexico. Tom Golder played in the Munich games. Other Victorians who reached the top were Jim Irvine, Colin Batch, Nigel Patmore, Wayne Thornton and Neil Snowden, all excellent players who contributed enormously to Australian Hockey and the glory of their great State of Victoria.

AUSTRALIA

My 'best ever' Australian side over the last thirty years would be as follows, with 'second best' shown as Reserve with each position:

Goal:
DEARING, Paul
(NSW)

Reserve:
REID, Graeme (ACT)

Backs:
IRVINE, Jim   GLENCROSS, Brian
(VIC)   (WA)

Reserves:
AGGIS, R (WA); DAVIES, C (WA)

Half Backs:

Right	*Centre*	*Left*
PEARCE, Gordon	PEARCE, Julian	HAIG, Robert
(WA)	(WA)	(SA)

Reserves:
BELL, David (WA); SMITH, Trevor (SA); KING, Treva (QLD)

Forwards:

Right Inside		*Left Inside*
CHARLSEWORTH, Ric		NILAN, Pat
(WA)		(NSW)

Right Wing	*Centre*	*Left Wing*
BROWNING, Greg	PEARCE, Eric	SMART, Don
(QLD)	(WA)	(WA)

Reserves:
BATCH, Colin (VIC); HASELHURST, Peter (WA); MITTON, Grant (SA);
RILEY, Ron (NSW); WALSH, Terry (WA)

CHAPTER SEVEN: ACT Hockey Association 1981-1984

In 1981, while I was working as Branch Manager for the English firm Gestetner in Melbourne, I applied to an advertisement in *Hockey Circle* (Australia's national hockey magazine) for the new position of Director of Coaching and Development for the ACT Hockey Association in Canberra.

I was quietly confident because I knew the people concerned had already been impressed by my work when I was Western Australian Junior Hockey Coach in 1973 and my team had won the Australian Junior Hockey Championships.

Sure enough, I received a phone call from the Honorary Secretary at the time, Les Gallagher, inviting me to fly to Canberra for an interview with Les himself and the President, Grant Waddell. The interview went well, and I was appointed to the position. My wife Jean and I, along with our young son David, who was 16 at the time, drove to Canberra from Melbourne on the last great adventure of my hockey career.

I took up the position in September 1981. My first task was to attract candidates from the hockey fraternity in Canberra. My aim was to build up a group of good coaches all preaching the same message, which would lighten the coaching load and spread the word more speedily. In order to achieve this I organized coaching seminars, which were extremely well received.

I invited high profile WA AIS coaches Dick Aggiss and

Brian Glencross to fly to Canberra to assist with the seminars. To my delight both of them eagerly accepted my invitation and their input was invaluable.

My next challenge was to persuade the Development Committee to part with a lot of money. Again, to my relief, my suggestion to purchase the needful was accepted. The Committee funded the purchase of machines for the production of small booklets on the various aspects of the job of coaching in the seminars and later in the clubs, and also the organising of coaching seminars at Coaching Levels 1 and 2.

My next project was the celebrated MINKEY, short for 'Mini Hockey'. We had the coaches, but we needed many kids for the programmes to come to fruition.

I started from scratch, canvassing primary schools in selected areas in Canberra. It was a tough task, but in the end I convinced numerous School Principals to agree to 30 minutes each week (one period) of hockey coaching in their schools, with the class teacher present to help with discipline. The objective was to spread the word about the modified rules that made the game more enjoyable for junior beginners.

I would front up at each school with a bag containing hockey sticks, balls, 'witches' hats (markers), bibs etc., all designed to get the kids simply to enjoy a game of hockey. I covered four schools a day and by the third week's stint we had recruited scores of kids to play on Saturday mornings in an organized way. We got the parents to drop off their kids for an hour while they went shopping or invited them to stay and watch their little ones play in a most enjoyable fashion.

The ugly spectre of money, of course, always loomed on the horizon. I solved this problem by approaching the ACT Milk Authority with a request for sponsorship. Their response was fantastic! We bought chocolate-flavoured and strawberry-flavoured milk from them with the money they gave us. We also imported small hockey sticks from India with Milk Authority Stickers on them and sold them at a very modest price so that parents did not have to pay inflated prices for the hockey sticks. The effect was electric! Parents had free baby-sitting, cheap exercise and a nourishing breakfast for their kids, all courtesy of MINKEY.

In time we moved to two other zones in Canberra and so in two years we grew from 12 teams to 130 teams, operating at three centres and feeding kids into the Club system. In fact a lot of clubs could not cope at first with this massive increase in numbers.

The success of our MINKEY programme was such that the South Australian Hockey Association requested me to come to Adelaide and show them how to run a MINKEY course for clubs in Adelaide, as many were not sold on this idea of Modified Rules Hockey. It didn't take long for the MINKEY message to take hold.

The introduction of a hockey unit into the Sports Study degree course at the Canberra College of Advanced Education exposed potential sports administrators, coaches and journalists to hockey and was one of the more memorable highlights of my work in Canberra.

Team preparation for National Championships was basically in the hands of the appointed coaches. I gave them much needed help by obtaining the good offices of Frank Pike in the assessing of fitness levels of the squad selected, so that Senior Coach John McKinnon could work on the data that the tests showed up in individuals. I personally accompanied the teams to Melbourne, Hobart and Perth.

Under the astute guidance of Brian Bowan the ACT Indoor team always gave a good account of themselves. Both Junior squads – Terry Dissledorf's U/17's and Bob Taylor's U/21's – both performed well above previous years and were a credit to their coaches and ACT over-all.

The word about my success with junior squads must have got around, because Louise Appleby, a senior official at the Education Department, and a schoolteacher Mrs Irene Forostenko requested the Men's Hockey Association to let me coach the Girls' team at the forthcoming tournament at Port Pirie (South Australia) and also at Campbelltown NSW.

I had never coached girls before. My only contact with girls' teams had hitherto been through MINKEY. Coaching my own girls' team turned out to be a most rewarding experience.

The outstanding player of that group was an eleven-year-old called Katrina Powell. She was magnificent! She scored goals, ran the opposition defences ragged and played with a skill level far above her age.

Katrina came from a Canberra hockey family that produced many great players. Her elder sister made the Australian Women's team before 'Trini' did. Then there was her uncle, who was a fine centre-half for the ACT Men's Senior team for many a year. All the Powells played for the Saint Pat's Hockey Club, a breeding ground for tough, skilful hockey players.

I predicted then that she would play for Australia and was delighted to see she duly did so and won Gold at two Olympics. At the time of writing this book she has been selected as Captain of the Australian Women's Hockey Team.

A lot of hard work that had started in the eighties finally came to fruition when Katrina Powell, my little twelve-year-old protégé from Canberra, was made Captain of the Australian Women's team. To me this was a special reward for the years of effort I had put in, and all the sacrifices my family had made.

I made a prediction about another young Canberran

who went on to play for Australia. Andrew Dean springs to mind. At the time Andrew was one of Terry Dissledorf's and Bob Taylor's stars. Andrew joined 1960 Olympian Errol Bill and great goalkeeper Graham Reid to represent Australia at National level from Australia's smallest hockey centre – ACT.

When the U/14 Boys' Championships were held in Canberra I was made Umpires' Director. To mark the occasion I bought a beautiful trophy from Kuala Lumpur and donated it to be used as the award for the best Junior Umpire of the tournament. This was a great incentive for these up-and-coming umpires, and was played for every year thereafter.

In order to foster Junior Coaching I arranged for several Senior players to visit Canberra and conduct coaching sessions for the kids. The first ones I called upon were Sydney Seniors Pat Nilan and Graeme Gilmore, both old friends from my Glebe Hockey Club days.

For another Level 2 Coaching Seminar in 1984 I called on old WA friends Frank Murray and Graeme (Butch) Worth to preside and be chief instructors at the seminar. Frank, of course, went on to be National Coach.

Although cigarette advertising in sport is now frowned upon, then it was accepted and even sought after as a source of very scarce funds. I approached the cigarette company Rothmans through a fellow Glebe hockey player called Bill Stubbs, who was a senior executive there. When my application was approved the ACT Hockey Association got a substantial sponsor's cheque.

Other people who gave me tremendous support while in Canberra were: Les and Marcia Gallagher, Brian Bowen, Malcolm Aldrons, Ray Brown, Martin Vitzjak, Billy Weidner, Bob Taylor, Bob Meridew, John McKinnon and Lynn Tagliari. There must be some names I have omitted for which I apologise.

It was with a heavy heart that I left Canberra in 1984 to rejoin my old firm Gestetner in Western Australia, but I knew in my soul that I had made a unique contribution to Australian hockey, especially in the time I had spent in Canberra. The friends I had made along the way were outstanding and remain irreplaceable. Thanks, Canberra, for some wonderful memories!

AUSTRALIAN PLAYERS 1922–1985

NAME	STATE	DATES
ABEL, J M	NSW	1922, 1923, 1925, 1927 (Test Captain)
ACTON, B	VIC	1950, 1952, 1954
AGGISS, R	WA	1969, 1970, 1971, 1974
ALLEN, J L	SA	1934, 1935 (Test Captain)
ALLEN, W D	SA	1935
ANDREW, R	WA	1967, 1970, 1971, 1972
ANNAND, B	VIC	1969
ANSTEY, C	Q	1937
ARNOTT, D	NSW	1923
AYLING, C B	NSW	1922
BALLARD, W	VIC	1937
BARBER, B	SA	1963
BARBLETT, A	WA	1955, 1956
BARNES, R	Q	1935, 1937
BARNES, A	Q	1948

BATCH, C	VIC	1979, 1980, 1981, 1982, 1983, 1984, 1985
BATES	NSW	1937
BEDFORD, L	WA	1967, 1969
BELL, D	WA	1975–1985(Test Capt.)
BELL, G	WA	1955, 1958, 1963, 1967
BENNETT, G	VIC	1956
BERCE, A	SA	1983–1985
BESLEY, F	VIC	1923
BEST, C	Q	1932, 1935, 1937
BESTALL, J	WA	1984, 1985
BICKFORD, H R	WA	1937
BILL, E	NSW	1960
BIRMINGHAM, W	NSW	1985
BLACKMORE, E	Q	1967
BOILEAU	VIC	1932
BOOTH, B	NSW	1956
BOYCE, G	WA	1977–1984
BRAY, W T	NSW	1923
BROWNE, F	WA	1948 Coach
BROWNING, G	Q	1969–1982

BUSCH, A	Q	1967–1969
BOURKE, B	WA	1970–1971
CARRIE, R	Q	1952
CARTON, K	WA	1955, 1956, 1960–1963
CHARLESWORTH, R	WA	1972–1985 (Test and Olympic Capt.)
CIBICH, B	SA	1977–1979
CIBICH, T	SA	1974
CLARK, F G	Q	1925
CLARKE, K	VIC	1956, 1958
CLARKE, R F	NSW	1950
COCKS, R J	NSW	1923
COOKE, I	NSW	1974–1981
COLLEGE, S	Q	1978, 1979, 1980, 1981, 1983, 1984, 1985
COOMBES, G	SA	1967
COOPER, D	Q	1943, 1950
CORMIE, C	Q	1929, 1932
CORMIE, H	Q	1927, 1929 (Test Capt.)
COULTER, E	Q	1929
CRAIG, A M	NSW	1922, 1923, 1925

CRAIG, M	VIC	1960 (Olympic Capt.)
CROSSMAN, M	Q	1960–1965
CULLEN, E	NSW	1934
CURRIE, D	Q	1958, 1961
CURRIE, J	Q	1961
DANCER, B	Q	1973–1979
DANE, J	TAS.	1950, 1952
DAVIES, C	WA	1978–1985
DEARING, P	NSW	1963–1970
DICK, I	WA	1948, 1950, 1952, 1954, 1956, 1958 (Test and Olympic Capt.)
DICK, R	TAS.	1977–1979
DICKIE, G M	WA	1932
DUNCAN, N	VIC	1963
DWYER, J	Q	1954, 1955, 1956, 1958
ELDER, K R	NSW	1922
ELLIS, J	Q	1961
ELLIOTT, J	NSW	1929, 1934
EVANS, R	WA	1960, 1961, 1963–1969
FERGUSON, N	Q	1927, 1929

FITZPATRICK, L K	NSW	1927, 1929
FLACK, B	NSW	1954
FLOCKHART, H J	NSW	1922, 1925, 1928
FLYNN, L	NSW	1983
FRANCIS, D	SA	1980–1985
FREEMAN, P B	NSW	1922
FRY, E H	NSW	1925
FOLEY, M	WA	1956
GARLICK, S	NSW	1937
GLENCROSS, D	SA	1967
GLENCROSS, B	WA	1964–1974 (Test and Olympic Capt.)
GIBLIN, J	SA	1967, 1969
GOLDER, T	VIC	1967, 1969, 1970, 1971, 1972, 1974, 1975, 1976
GRANT, D N	NSW	1954, 1958
GRANT, W A	NSW	1922, 1925, 1927, 1929
GRAY, J E	NSW	1956
GREEN, W	Q	1974–1982
HAILEY, L	Q	1955, 1958, 1960
HAIGH, R	SA	1966–1976 (Test Capt.)

HAMMOND, W	Q	1972, 1973, 1981
HANCOCK, R	WA	1940
HART, V	NSW	1932
HARRY, C A	NSW	1922
HASELHURST, P	WA	1978–1985
HATTER, A	NSW	1934
HAYWOOD, S	WA	1983, 1984
HAZELTON, R	NSW	1961, 1962
HODDER, R	VIC	1963–1967
HOWELL, R	VIC	1967
HUDSON, W	NSW	1929
HUDSON, M	NSW	1952, 1954
HUGHES, K M	NSW	1922
HURRELL, G	NSW	1937
HURRELL, J	NSW	1935, 1937
IRVINE, J	VIC	1969, 1973–1985
IRVINE, A	NSW	1934
JOHNSON, G	NSW	1956, 1958
JOHNSON, E	Q	1948
JOSIFFE, H	Q	1948
KEMP, D A	WA	1954, 1956
KENDALL, V M	NSW	1922, 1925
KENNEDY, F	WA	1948

KERR, J	Q	1932
KING, T	Q	1978, 1980–1985
KIRK, R	WA	1961
LAVERLY, J	NSW	1950
LEE, A	NSW	1954 (Test Capt.)
LEE, T	NSW	1929 (Tour Capt.)
LEECE, T	WA	1981–1984
LEGGETT, C	NSW	1934
LE LIEVRE, K	NSW	1934
LIVERSIDGE, P	VIC	1974
LOVETT, K	NSW	1955
MAHONEY, J	Q	1935, 1937 (Test Capt.)
MALCOLM, B	Q	1960
MALLISON, A	TAS.	1958
MARSHALL, S	SA	1969, 1973, 1974, 1975, 1976
MARTIN, D	WA	1961, 1963, 1966, 1968
MASON, J	Q	1967–1974
MAY, L G	VIC	1983
MAY, R E	VIC	1922, 1923
McASKELL, T	VIC	1967, 1969, 1970, 1971, 1972, 1973,

		1974 (test Capt.)
McBRIDE, J	Q	1961–1965 (Test and Olympic Capt.)
McBRIDE, I	Q	1969
McCORMACK, J	NSW	1961–1966
McINTOSH, K	NSW	1958
McKENZIE, F	WA	1935
McLENNAN, R	VIC	1969, 1970
McNAMARA, B	Q	1948, 1950
McNEIL, W	NSW	1932
McWATTERS, D	Q	1961–1968 (Test and Olympic Capt.)
MECKLIN, D	Q	1955, 1956, 1958 (Test Capt.)
MILLER, J	NSW	1925
MILLER, H	VIC	1935
MILNER, G F	WA	1932, 1934, 1935, 1937 (Test Capt.)
MILNER, R	NSW	1923
MILLS, J S	NSW	1925
MINTO, G	VIC	1934
MITTON, D	SA	1958
MITTON, G	SA	1980, 1981, 1983, 1984
MOIR, A J	VIC	1932

MONFRIES, B E	NSW	1935
MORLEY, C M	VIC	1948 (Test Capt. and Coach)
MULLINS, J	Q	1955, 1958
MUNROWD, D	WA	1950
MURRAY, W R	NSW	1950, 1952
NETTLETON, W E	NSW	1923, 1925, 1927, 1929
NEWTON, M	NSW	1935
NICKLIN, S R	NSW	1922
NILAN, P	NSW	1961, 1964–1970, 1972
NIMMO, R H	VIC	1927
NOEL, P	SA	1985
NOBBS, M	SA	1979–1985
O'RIELLY, M	WA	1967
OGG, P	Q	1927
OXLEY, A E	VIC	1927
PARRY, R	SA	1969, 1970, 1971, 1973
PATMORE, N	VIC	1982–1982
PEARCE, C	WA	1950, 1952, 1954, 1955, 1956, 1958
PEARCE, E	WA	1955, 1956, 1960, 1962, 1964, 1965,

		1966
PEARCE, M G	WA	1952, 1955, 1956
PEARCE, J	WA	1960, 1962, 1964, 1965, 1966, 1968, 1970
PEARCE, T	NSW	1937
PERMAN, K	Q	1934
PETTY, E	Q	1927
PHILLIPS, G	NSW	1969, 1970
PIPER, D	VIC	1962–1964, 1966–1972
PITT, I	SA	1966
POINTON, W J	NSW	1937, 1948
POOLE, M	WA	1973–1980
PRATT, S	TAS	1983
PRITCHARD, P	WA	1960
PROCTOR	NSW	1974–1979
PROSSER, A J	WA	1935, 1937
PULLY, A	NSW	1929
QUINE, F	Q	1961, 1968
READ, K	TAS	1978
REECE, T A	NSW	1954
REID, G	ACT	1970, 1974, 1976–1982

REID, G	Q	1984–1985
REID, K	Q	1955–1956
REID, L	NSW	1934
REEVE, M	TAS	1963
REYNOLDS, W C	SA 1952	
RICH, T	NSW	1967
RICHARDS, P	TAS	1973–1974
RILEY, H A	NSW	1927
RILEY, R	NSW	1967, 1968, 1970, 1972, 1973, 1975, 1976, 1977, 1979, 1980
ROBERTSON, W C	WA	1932
ROBSON, H	Q	1969
ROGERS, J F	NSW	1922
ROTHWELL, E	NSW	1934
ROTHWELL, W	NSW	1922 (Player Manager)
ROURKE, B	WA	1974
RODDA, J	SA	1985
SALISBURY, B	Q	1948
SANDY, J	VIC	1967
SAUNDERS, H	NSW	1923
SCHULTE, A	Q	1948

SCOTT, S	Q	1935, 1937
SEAMAN, S A	NSW	1922, 1925
SIGGS, D	Q	1948, 1950, 1952 (Test Capt.)
SMART, D	WA	1961, 1963–1972
SMITH, H J	WA	1950, 1952
SMITH, R	NSW	1927
SMITH, Roger	SA	1980–1985
SMITH, Trevor	SA	1971, 1974–1984
SMITH, Terry	SA	1975, 1979
SMITH, S	WA	1977, 1978, 1979
SNOWDEN, N	VIC	1980–1985
SODEN, S G	Q	1925
SONTER, B K	Q	1954
SOUTHWOOD, E	WA	1948
SPACKMAN, D	NSW	1955, 1956, 1958, 1960
SPEDDING, I	NSW	1958
SPEDDING, K	NSW	1958
STENNING, M	NSW	1934
STEPHEN, K	VIC	1985
STEPHENS, S	NSW	1934
STEPHENS, S	NSW	1929

STEPHENSON, L R	NSW	1950, 1952, 1954
STRAUSS, R B	WA	1954
TART, B	NSW	1927, 1934
TAYLOR, S	NSW	1927
TESTER, P	NSW	1934
THORNTON, K	VIC	1948, 1950
THORNTON, W	VIC	1980–1981
TODD, E	SA	1950
TODKILL, W	NSW	1927, 1929
TREGONNING, D	WA	1932 (Test Capt.)
VAN ASSCHE, I	VIC	1932
WANLESS, W	NSW	1932
WARK, K E	NSW	1952, 1954
WARK, K	NSW	1985
WALSH, T	WA	1974–1984
WALTER, G	WA	1974–1975
WATERS, T	WA	1961, 1964, 1965
WATSON, N	Q	1934, 1935
WEBB, S	TAS	1973
WESTRUP, R C	VIC	1952
WHITESIDE, R	VIC	1956
WILDMAN, W	NSW	1983
WILLOTT, P	NSW	1965–1967

WILLIAMS, A	TAS	1967
WILMOTT, S	Q	1923
WILSON, R	WA	1970, 1972
WINSTON, D F	Q	1952, 1954, 1958
WISE, D	Q	1948, 1952
WOOD, G	VIC	1960, 1963, 1964, 1965
WOOD, O P	NSW	1923
WRIGHT, R A	NSW	1952, 1954

AUSTRALIAN UNDER 21 TEAM PLAYERS 1981–1985

NAME	STATE	DATES
ANASTASIOU, A	VIC	1983
ANDREWS, A	VIC	1981
BATTY, P	Q	1981, 1982
BELL, A	WA	1983
BESTALL, J	WA	1981–1984
BUTCHER, B	TAS	1983–1984
BIRMINGHAM, W	NSW	1982
CARISTENSEN, S	SA	1981
COLLEGE, S	Q	1981
DE MAN, P	VIC	1981
DALTON, S	VIC	1984
DIPNALL, M	VIC	1981, 1982, 1984
FAIRBROTHER, C	VIC	1981, 1982 (Capt.)
FITZPATRICK, S	NSW	1982–1984
GALANOS, J	VIC	1981–1982
GASPARINI, O	SA	1981–1982
HAGER, M	Q	1983–1984
HARPER, R	VIC	1982–1984
HEMERY, M	WA	1982–1983
HOPKINS, D	WA	1984
HYMUS, G	WA	1984

JOHNSON, D	WA	1983–1984
LOMAS, I	Q	1983
LOVE, C	SA	1983–1984
MITTON, G	SA	1981–1982
MORGAN, W	NSW	1982
NINNESS, J	NSW	1984
NOEL, P	SA	1982–1984
PATMORE, N	VIC	1981
PAVITT, I	Q	1981
PRATT, S	TAS	1981
READ, Graham	Q	1983–1984
READ, Greg	VIC	1984
SAUNDERS, D	TAS	1982
SHAW, P	Q	1981–1982
SMITH, R	SA	1981 (Capt.)
WILSDEN, B	SA	1983
WONG, R	ACT	1983
ZEKULICH, B	WA	1982–1984 (Capt.)

About the Author

Trevor Vanderputt was born in India and was educated by the Irish Christian Brothers. He learned his Hockey on the sub-continent and played First Division for Calcutta Rangers Club in the 50's. Served as a Bengal Senior Selector with Keshav Dutt and Balbir Kapoor.

Emigrated to Australia in 1964 with his wife Jean and four sons. Though over the hill age-wise to play top grade, played with Glebe H.C in Sydney and Cricketers Club in Perth. Wide experience in coaching Club and State sides in Australia. Was appointed Director of Coaching in the Hockey Association in Canberra. Worked for the English Office Equipment Company, Gestetner, over a period of 40 years. Finished as State Manager, Western Australia and ran his own Company for 6 years before retiring. Now lives in Perth and will celebrate his 50th year of marriage in February 2003.